Feminine
Mysteries
in the
Bible

Feminine
Mysteries
in the
Bible

*The Soul Teachings of
the Daughters of the Goddess*

Ruth Rusca

Bear & Company
Rochester, Vermont

Bear & Company
One Park Street
Rochester, Vermont 05767
www.BearandCompanyBooks.com

Bear & Company is a division of Inner Traditions International

Library of Congress Cataloging-in-Publication Data
Rusca, Ruth, 1929–
  Feminine mysteries in the Bible : the soul teachings of the daughters of the goddess / Ruth Rusca.
    p. cm.
  Includes bibliographical references and index.
  ISBN 978-1-59143-088-9 (pbk.)
  1. Women in the Bible. 2. Bible. O.T.—Feminist criticism. 3. Bible. O.T.—Miscellanea. I. Title.

BS575.R78 2008
220.9'2082—dc22

                                                                2008025992

Printed and bound in the United States by Lake Book Manufacturing

10 9 8 7 6 5 4 3 2 1

Text design and layout by Carol Ruzicka
This book was typeset in Garamond with Italian Electric as a display typeface

To send correspondence to the author of this book, mail a first-class letter to the author c/o Inner Traditions • Bear & Company, One Park Street, Rochester, VT 05767, and we will forward the communication.

This book is dedicated to my grandchildren,
Una, Otis, and Emilia,
and to my celestial friends

Contents

Part One

Mythic Dimensions of the Historical Periods
of the Four Women

Part Two

The Stories of Tamar, Rahab, Ruth, and Bathsheba:
A Symbolic Interpretation

Part Three

The Conception of Mary:
A Symbolic Interpretation of the Apocryphal Legend

Foreword

I am honored to have been invited by my dear friend Ruth Rusca to write this brief foreword to the marvelous book you are about to read.

Ruth's study of the four women from the Hebrew Bible whom the gospel of Matthew lists as foremothers of Jesus is the culmination of an almost lifelong task, one that has cost her much in the way of pain, sacrifice, and solitude. In a sense it had its beginnings in Ruth's childhood exposure to the rich symbolism of the Catholic liturgy that surrounded her as a Protestant child growing up in Italian-speaking southern Switzerland, an exposure that led her from early on to respond to religious symbols as symbols. Then in midlife, shortly after undergoing a hysterectomy, she experienced an imperative calling to shift her energy to spiritual creativity and suddenly and mysteriously found herself drawn to the myth of Mary's immaculate conception. As you will see, her understanding of what this really meant has continued to deepen during the almost twenty-five years that have since passed.

Quite early Ruth had an intuition that to understand Mary she needed to understand her relation to her foremothers, to understand her as a *daughter*, and not just as mother. She surmised that the inclusion of Tamar, Rahab, Ruth, and Bathsheba in Matthew's genealogy implies a (perhaps unconscious) recognition that an exclusively male lineage for the savior will not serve. Of course in the gospel all four women are named *as mothers*—Tamar of Pharez, Rahab of Boaz, Ruth of Obed, Bathsheba of Solomon—and in Matthew the lineage ends with Joseph (not Mary!).

But Ruth's interpretation is transgressive; it goes beyond the text. For her it is not as mothers that these women enter the story but as powerful, initiative-taking, sexual women. She is deeply aware that the reemergence of the Goddess energy, the feminine energy, rejected in patriarchal monotheism is necessarily a transgressive move, beautifully symbolized by the stories involving these four women—each of whom came from outside the Hebrew world (Tamar and Rahab were Canaanites, Ruth a Moabite, and Bathsheba a Hittite).

As her book makes clear, this revisioning of Mary by way of her transgressive foremothers is intended to help all of us, men as well as women, move toward a more holistic consciousness. Ruth is deeply aware of the cost to all of us of our culture's domination by the differentiating consciousness often designated as "masculine," though she is also appreciative of its historical and psychological necessity. Indeed, she is hoping to help us move beyond the polarizing of the masculine and feminine, of spirit and matter, of soul and sexuality, which encourages us to see them as opposites, as intrinsically incompatible.

By entering deeply into these stories, Ruth seeks to make visible their relevance to our own soul journeys and to the overcoming of these tensions in ourselves. She notes how the sexuality of each of the four women led to their becoming part of the biblical story. She emphasizes how all but Bathsheba took conscious initiative and assumed responsibility for her exercise of power. Bathsheba, in contrast, was passive in relation to King David: she allowed herself to be abducted by him and did not take responsibility for her seductive sexual beauty. (Still, I do want to add that later on Bathsheba took a lot of initiative in tricking David into naming her son, Solomon, as his heir—though, granted, even that is the use of feminine wile, not forthright exercise of power.)

In any case Ruth sees Bathsheba not as a model for us, but—precisely in her weakness—serving as a call to us to complete a pattern she herself leaves unfinished.

Not too surprisingly perhaps, the most moving exploration is the one focused on the biblical Ruth, the author's own namesake, who has come to be "an invisible friend," who "lives uninhibitedly in order to make a relationship fruitful and to stay true to her innermost self." Ruth Rusca sees that Ruth essentially as a *daughter*, as remaining Naomi's daughter even after literally bearing a child, since she immediately turns her son over to Naomi to raise. This becomes an even more central theme when she turns to Mary, since she sees the story of the Immaculate Conception as providing us with a Mary who is also not primarily a mother but a daughter.

For what is most important about Ruth Rusca's powerful innovative study is that it is adamantly not calling for a return to the Mother Goddess and the undifferentiated consciousness she represents. Just as in Christian mythology God the Father incarnates in a human son, so the archaic Mother Goddess needed to incarnate in a human daughter. So Mary is important not as a future mother of Jesus or as a virgin, but as a fully human, truly embodied, deeply feminine, individualized daughter of the Goddess.

Thus in the first version of this study the conception of Mary was seen as representing the goal of the feminine journey; Mary was the distillation of the "four energy streams" flowing from her transgressive foremothers. The goal of our soul journeys was the conception of this powerful Mary in us, in our souls.

But the study had not yet been completed after all. For, seven years after Ruth thought she was done, she found herself having to add a chapter on the Magdalene. She had come to see that the two Marys together actually more fully represent the archetype of female human wholeness than either could on her own. The tradition of seeing Mary of Nazareth only in her motherly and virginal aspects may be too well established. In Mary of Magdala the integration of the sexual and the spiritual, the active and the receptive, is more readily seen.

So in the end I, too, am grateful for the delay—and even more grateful that now at last this wonderful book is ready for its readers.

CHRISTINE DOWNING

Christine Downing, Ph.D., is currently a professor of Mythological Studies at Pacifica Graduate Institute in Santa Barbara. She was the first woman president of the American Academy of Religion, the primary professional association for religious studies scholars. She taught for almost twenty years in the Department of Religious Studies at San Diego State University and, during the same period, was a member of the Core Faculty at the San Diego campus of the California School of Professional Psychology. From 1963 to 1974 she served as a faculty member of the Religion Department at Douglass College of Rutgers University. She has also taught at the Jung Institute in Zurich and lectures frequently to Jungian groups, both in the United States and abroad, and at American and European universities. She is the author of *The Goddess: Mythological Images of the Feminine, Psyche's Sisters: Reimaging the Meaning of Sisterhood, Women's Mysteries: Towards a Poetic Gender,* and *The Long Journey Home: Reinvisioning the Myth of Demeter and Persephone for Our Time.*

Acknowledgments

My deep thanks goes to my life companion of 54 years, Gianni, who sustained me through the decades of my research with great love and generosity, and to my children Bettina, Nicola, and Andrea, who supported and accepted me, although I was not always an easy mother. I am grateful to Christine Downing, to whom I owe the courage to write my book in English, which is not my mother tongue, as well as her endorsement to bring the book to publication. My gratitude goes to Cielle Tewksbury for her untiring patience, indulgence, and love to correct my imperfect English. My thanks to Mirella Giuliano, who always brought me back to solid ground when I floated in the clouds of illusion; she gave my tentative steps in writing some structure. My thankfulness also goes to all my travel companions who always believed in the work we were doing. I would like to thank Chungliang Al Huang for teaching me how much joy of life is in the Tai'ji dance. I have Antonio Tironi to thank for the most profound conversations that always ended with mirth and laughter. A heartfelt thank you to Juan Nuñez del Prado, who foretold that my book would be published—he was the most mysterious encounter in my life and helped me to experience the powerful and lively presence of Pachamama. I am grateful for the caring support and the sensitive editing of the staff at Inner Traditions, Bear & Company, of my work. And finally, I'm grateful to Barbara Bruppacher for acting as a very competent liaison between the publisher and me.

─◄○►─

How This Book Came to Be

Although I was born into a German-speaking Protestant family, I grew up in the Catholic, Italian-speaking environment of a small village, my hometown, where the sacred and the profane existed side by side. Our Easter celebrations were feasts in which the whole village took part. Women and young girls were busy for months in advance, creating new dresses or altering old ones to wear to Mass on Easter morn. I recall reciting fifty Ave Maria's in Latin every evening for a whole month, praying for fair weather on the special day. I can still remember the smell of the earth and hear the hundreds of swallows announcing spring, the time of new life and rebirth.

I did not realize it at the time, but I was allowed the freedoms of the Protestant religion while feeling the fascination and the stir of the symbols of Catholicism. My religious education was free and unrestricted, unconditioned by religious creeds from either denomination. But that wasn't true for everyone. I recall that my dearest childhood friend was very upset and worried that I would be condemned to burn in hell because I was not baptized in the Catholic Church. She was also rebuked in a Sunday sermon for bathing with me in the river, an act considered indecent for girls at that time.

I lived through a childhood close to nature and the cyclic movements of the seasons, which gave me the precious gift of a sense of oneness and continuity. At the same time, I had the feeling that I was a foreigner, one who lived in an "in-between" world. I peopled this world with kings, queens, princes, and princesses, and with children like myself, children who belonged to neither world, German or Italian, Protestant or Catholic, and who felt lonely and orphaned. This "in-between" world gave me a sense of security, a place where I felt at home. In my innocence I did not know that this land was the realm of the soul, the place where contrasts cease. I later learned that when we consciously integrate such contrasts and contradictions, we create a deep new sense of meaning, unity, and wholeness.

The most fateful challenge that I encountered in my life came in the form of the Immaculate Conception, celebrated by the Catholic Church every year on the eighth of December. This celebration is based on the belief that Mary, the mother of Jesus, was free from the stain of original sin that, in the official Catholic view, has been passed down from Adam to every other human being, transmitted by sexual acts.[1] At the same time, she was conceived and born through the union of Anna and Joachim, her human parents. After being elaborated and distilled for centuries, this belief was officially declared an infallible dogma by Pius IX in 1854. Although it is generally confused with the belief in the virginal conception and birth of Jesus, in this dogma, the Church defined the doctrine that, from the moment of her conception, Mary was *untainted by original sin.*

After a conversation with a Franciscan monk, questions concerning the Immaculate Conception and its message for today became embedded in my heart. I came to see this dogma as an example of the repression of the divine feminine in Christianity. As a woman of forty, with a husband and three children, I began a quest for understanding, impelled by an imperative urge to follow an inner call. It became my life task, a task that brought enrichment interwoven with pain, sacrifice, and solitude. This book is a distillation, the result of many years of research conducted privately and with groups of women, both of which contributed to a deepening of my understanding.

It became clear to me that the dogma of the Immaculate Conception is a symbol of the essence of soul experience and not a physical truth. It expresses the quintessence of a greater truth, a hidden mystery of life, which we must approach with humility and respect. C. G. Jung speaks of the negative connotation of the word *dogma,* because it speaks in a language that has become foreign to the modern spirit. It has come to indicate inflexibility and prejudice, and for most Western people it has lost its original significance as a symbol of an unknowable yet actual, operative fact.

The dogma of the Immaculate Conception contains a profound feminine mystery, which has been given a Christological response that overlooks the humanness of Mary, viewing her exclusively as the pure, virginal mother of Jesus. From a feminine standpoint, however, this dogma speaks above all about the birth of a *daughter,* conceived under miraculous circumstances by human parents. This event has been portrayed in the legend of "Natività di Maria" of the *Vangeli apocrifi Natività e infanzia* to compensate for what has been excluded from the Bible and the Church. I will relate this legend at the end of this work, because I discovered that the conception of Mary is the final goal of a long journey of the feminine soul and, at the same time, marks a new beginning.

> We shall not cease from exploration
> And the end of all our exploring
> Will be to arrive where we started
> And know the place for the first time.[2]

We begin to weave our future personal myths when we are children, unconsciously following the blueprint of our destiny. It is the privilege of aging to see life from a broader perspective. This enables us to recognize purpose and meaning as well as all the detours we take as we try to elude the inevitable, to escape the inexorability of a greater power. This power brings us to the gateway where we "shed" our old selves and, ultimately, our physical body of this lifetime, like the serpent, whose shedding of skin is the oldest symbol of the mysterious renewal of life.

In my own personal exploration of symbol and myth I found an intimate link between the Immaculate Conception and the Old Testament, which also portrays the repression of the divine feminine. Joseph Campbell discusses this rejection of the Goddess in historical terms. His explanation is based on the occupation of Canaan by the Hebrews and their subjugation of its people. The principal divinity of the Canaanites was the Goddess; her animal symbol was the serpent. Both the Goddess and her symbol were rejected by the Hebrews.

In a patriarchal world, the experience of the divine in feminine form is not incarnated into human life. The rejected Goddess can only reemerge through transgressions. In a moral sense, to transgress means "to violate a law, an order"; in Latin, *transgredi* simply means "to go beyond." In the story of the Garden of Eden, not only the Goddess and the serpent, but also the Tree of Life are rejected. In Genesis 2:9, we are told about two trees in the center of the garden; the Tree of Life and the Tree of Knowledge (of good and evil). The serpent offered Eve the fruit of the Tree of Knowledge. After the Fall, *the first transgression,* we read the following phrase:

> And the Lord God said, Behold, the man is become as one of us to know good and evil: and now, lest he put forth his hand, and take also of the tree of life, and eat, and live forever. . . . (Genesis 3:22)

The Bible states that God placed cherubim and a flaming sword by the Tree of Life to guard and protect it. This flaming blade becomes the cutting edge of differentiation. It becomes evident that original sin is the fall into the duality of good and evil. It represents the experience of the divine in its masculine form, that is, "becoming one of us, knowing good and evil." With the assertion of the masculine divine, the feminine was suppressed.

It is not possible to eliminate a divine energy, however, and the Bible itself tells part of the story of how the Goddess reemerges in her transcendent dimensions, in her totality. In Matthew 1:1–6, amid the mention of many generations of forefathers, the genealogical tree of Jesus makes mention of four foremothers as well as Mary. Their surprising presence bears witness to the continuity of symbolic, mythic life. What was it about these particular women that led to their inclusion in the list? The answer lies in their capacity to hand down from woman to woman, from generation to generation, an indestructible, transgressive, feminine life force, a force with enough strength to carve its way through a patriarchal world of law and order.

The four women and the books of the Bible where their stories appear are:

Tamar Genesis 38
Rahab Joshua 2, 6
Ruth   Book of Ruth
Bathsheba   II Samuel 11, 12; I Kings 1

These stories teach us how to recognize ourselves in a fourfold feminine life process, for they symbolize the four stages of the development of soul consciousness. The four stages could be described as follows:

Tamar is dealing with the masculine world through her instinct. When a woman begins to listen to her soul it usually has its beginning through becoming paradoxically more conscious of the body and sexuality in building up an identity separated from the masculine principle but in relation with it.

The biblical *Rahab* is confronted in this stage with the mythical Rahab, named Chaos, Dragon, the wild one. Her task is a very difficult one, because this time she has to separate her identity from the Great Mother. She needs all the male forces she has conquered in the first stages to become a daughter, but at the same time she has to save feminine cultural values expressed in using the language of the soul. The cultural feminine values symbolize the eternal indestructible link to the Goddess that in spite of the autonomy of the daughter remains.

Ruth represents the ability to bring down to earth the experience of the feminine soul to be a daughter. Not only the daughter of the Goddess but of both united divine parents.

Bathsheba, the daughter of the Goddess, would be able to transmit on a collective level the soul teaching of the united divine, thus to become a spiritual reality in human beings.

The stories are linked together as if a spiraling thread were running through them, and they become complete only when each is considered as part of the whole. They find their fulfillment in Mary, who is the quintessence of the four.

C. G. Jung speaks of all quaternal numbers as symbols relating to the process of becoming conscious of completeness, of the fundamental oneness of all reality. The number four seems to correspond to an archetypal basic structure in the human psyche. Jung has given an immense significance to the number four. He says that it seems to correspond to a typical archetypal psychic ground structure disposition in human beings that is oriented to wholeness, which has quaternal character.[3]

All over the world in many cultures we found those fourfold models in the Divinity. It seems to me that the fourfold stages of development of soul consciousness to completeness expressed by the four women correspond to the idea of archetypal fourfold soul disposition mentioned by Jung in many of his books; but as far as I know not in relation to the feminine soul. There is some parallel in the book series of Robert Moore and Douglas Gillette concerning the fourfold structure of the male psyche: *King, Warrior, Magician, and Lover Within.*

In this sense the four women represent, through their life stories, the stepping-stones to completeness. They speak to us, in spite of the dominant presence of God the Father, of the experience of the divine in feminine form.

The first experience of the divine in its masculine form is an experience of separation, as we see in the story of the Garden of Eden. This experience divided the female nature: one part became physical and despicable, the other spiritual and unobtainable. Thus, when the feminine power reemerges in a world dominated by men, it is forced to violate a masculine law. It has to move beyond a sterile, one-sided, restrictive vision of life. So it is not surprising that the four foremothers of Jesus share a "sacred prostitute" or "harlot priestess" nature. Feminist author Barbara Walker defines "holy virgin" as the harlot priestess of Ishtar and of Aphrodite. The title did not mean one who possessed physical virginity, but rather one who was "unwed."

> The function of such "holy virgins" was to dispense the Mother's grace through sexual worship; to heal; to prophesy; to perform sacred dances; to wail for the dead; and to become Brides of God.[4]

In Canaan, Babylon, and Palestine they were called *kadesha,* which means "holy one," and this is the title given to Tamar in Genesis 38:21. In the Italian Pontifical Bible (*La Sacra Bibbia*), however, Tamar is instead referred to as a "public woman," and, as the term indicates, one of those "wretched women" who exposed themselves to the public lust in the temples of "obscene" pagan cults. This statement reflects the profound separation between the sexual and the sacred nature of women. The sacred prostitute's sexual nature has been rejected and split off from the image of Mary. But Mary was also once called *kadesha.* The Catholic Church has created an image of the Virgin purified of sensual, joyful sexuality, divorced from her instinctual feminine ground. It is an image that conforms to the masculine experience.

But for a woman, these two elements are never separated. For many women, the image of the sacred prostitute, the Holy Virgin, the harlot priestess, expresses most unequivocally the mystery of the oneness of body and spirit through the soul. In her book, *The Sacred Prostitute,* Nancy Qualls-Corbett states:

Yet the sacred prostitute remains a mystery, in large part because our modern attitude makes it difficult for us to grasp what we see as a paradox in her image: her sexual nature was an integral aspect of her spiritual nature. For most of us that conjunction is a contradiction. In ancient times, however, it was a unity.[5]

Out of sexual union evolve the experiences of conception, pregnancy, birth, and nursing, which are physical as well as sacred processes for women that men do not share in. In this light, the sacred prostitute becomes the bride of God. She is the physical vessel containing the divine dimension, expressing the mystery of sacred marriage and the possibility of new life, both physically and psychologically. It is the sexual act, which overcomes duality, wherein two become one. This is the ecstasy of orgasm, a moment in time when the boundaries of egos collapse and the divine unity can manifest. It is the most direct physical avenue to divine manifestation and as such, the most overwhelming.

It is not surprising that humankind has erected taboos and rituals around the sexual act. But when it is split off from matter to become "free of original sin," which is the intention of the church in its dogma of the Immaculate Conception, it has lost its oneness. The Vatican still condemns sexuality as a sin when not practiced within the sacred bond of matrimony, and even then only for the purpose of procreation.

Can we grasp the meaning of the sacred prostitute with our modern outlook? She is the vessel of the indestructible life force; she mediates between the human and the divine. She is the link to our instinctual roots. She is the keeper of the wisdom of the Goddess. She is the teacher of the transformative power of the soul. She is the unity of body and spirit made manifest. She embodies love. In and of herself, she is the One. She is a soul-teacher. Barbara Walker, in her book *The Woman's Encyclopedia of Myths and Secrets,* informs us that the holy virgins or temple harlots were *alma mater:* "soul-teachers" or "soul-mothers." The word *alma* means "the living soul of the world," identical to the Greek *psyche* and the Sanskrit *shakti.* In many old songs and verses, Mary is still called the Alma Mater. We have lost our soul-teachers; the image of God has lost its female soul, once represented by Sophia (in the Gnostic view), the source of his power and the spirit of female wisdom. This schism and the ensuing loss have damaged our lives and the life of our Mother Earth and all her creatures.

The feminine life force, the serpent power, can be deadly as well as life transforming, depending on our awareness of it. This can be seen in the way we often attach a negative, death-bringing interpretation to a powerful divine gift. My daughter reported the following dream to me at the time I was writing about this issue. In the dream, I was giving her a little, newborn baby that she knew was her own. In reality, my daughter is not able to have a physical child; the child in the dream represents the recognition and acknowledgment of her intuitive gift. In her daily life, her friends tease her for this aptitude, calling her a "witch."

The collective layer of fear and negative projection on gifted and powerful women is perpetuated by myth as well as in our consciousness. But it is possible for us to change our attitude. A current example of this may be found in Christa Wolf's book, *Medea,* in which she moves beyond the classical interpretation to reveal a powerful, gifted Medea who never killed her brother or her children. A gift of profound intuition is one of the ways we can experience the divine in feminine form as an unconscious or conscious legacy of the Goddess.

I have been deeply influenced by this feminine life force, feeling it slowly growing upward, organically, like a tree rising out of my instinctual ground. Riding lessons were my entrée to the world of instinct. I experienced in rare moments the beauty of the sense of unity when the rider's commands are met by the animal's willingness to surrender to them. Then the rider and horse are as one. At other times, however, the horse was the expert, and when *I* did not surrender, I felt the soft, loving guidance of the horse coming to meet me halfway. It is important to become aware of our inner motherly soul garden where the Tree of Life has its roots. As with the horse and its rider, instinctual impulses may throw us to the ground, but when honored, acknowledged, and heeded, they become our faithful helpers, like many animals in fairy tales.

This same life force has been transmitted in many inspiring ways by the current research of women, mothers, and sisters in spirit, creating a strong bond of kinship as we recognize our common instinctual feminine roots. This connection is symbolized by the motif of the red thread, which, as we shall see, appears in the stories of all four women mentioned in the genealogical tree of Jesus. In this symbol we cradle our deep and ancient lost identity: our blood relationship with the Goddess.

However, reclaiming that identity doesn't have to be based on a rejection of the masculine divine. Although we can look at the Garden of Eden from a dualistic point of view, which takes cognizance of the polar nature of the two trees, one of life and one of knowledge, we can also regard it from a holistic standpoint, in which the Tree of Life shelters good and evil, life and death, masculine and feminine. Goethe once said that to find yourself in eternity, you have to differentiate and then unite.

> *Dich im Unendlichen zu finden*
> *Musst unterscheiden und dann verbinden.*[6]

Finding a parallel in our personal lives lends meaning to these Biblical stories. At one period in our women's group, we had reached a plateau of harmony that became stagnant. We all knew that a beautiful period of togetherness was ending, and we all had to define our lives and tasks anew. It was a painful but necessary separation, and it was a time to make room for new vistas to unfold. The sense of oneness and harmony we all felt was the experience of the divine in feminine form. The painful but clearly indicated separation was the flaming sword, the experience of the divine in its masculine form, a necessary step on the path of consciousness and individuation. It was a fruitful decision. Our lives now flow more freely in different directions, and we are all aware of the thread holding us together in a new way.

As human beings, we all have many "Garden of Eden" moments in our lives, when our serpent instinct impels us to eat from the fruit of a new awareness. It forces us to transform and encourages us to shed our old skin and to renew our life. In this way we discover our soul garden. There is a unifying life force that always leads us back to our source, to our Tree of Life. Collectively, it is time for us all to stretch out our hands and grasp the fruit of the Tree of Life, that is, to reconnect with the eternal, primal energy, but with a new experience and a new awareness of both sides of the divine.

We yearn to be reunited with our souls. Throughout the years I have worked on the theme of the four biblical women, I have experienced them as my own soul-teachers: powerful, wise guides along the sacred road of life. In acknowledging the priest as the God's designated delegate in the tending of the soul, we exclude the Goddess-delegate, the priestess as soul-teacher. The Vatican has declared that women will never stand before the altar, because the priestess represents an archetypal female pattern, which stirs up powerful images of temple harlots and sacred prostitutes. However, the feminine dimension of the divine is now reemerging all over the world in many creative men and women as a unifying energy to overcome the stagnation of the soul. We have to violate our antiquated belief systems and patterns to assure the continuity of the life of the soul. We must also leave behind old beliefs whose time has long gone, which threaten our planet on a physical level.

One summer day I was sitting with my pilgrimage companions atop the highest hill on the island of Iona, near the well that is called "Eternal Youth," the "Ageless Place." From this vantage point, we viewed the splendor of the entire island, the turquoise sea and the blue sky meeting together in a breath. Down on the green pastures beneath us, many sheep were being herded out of a gate by a shepherd and his dog. We could see what infinite patience it took to herd them, again and again, in the right direction. It was amazing to see them all in a row, overseen by the dog, running along their narrow path as if pulled by an invisible thread. After a long night of enduring their continuous bleating, we discovered they had been rounded up to be slaughtered the next morning. In a sudden moment of illumination, I saw the parallel to our own life and what a difference it makes if we can regard it with awareness and compassion, embracing our whole existence with its shadows and light, failures and successes, rather than being driven unconsciously along in fear and pain to our physical end. This awareness originates in the soul, the ageless place, the never-dying link to the divine eternal source of life.

Mystical understanding has its source in the soul, but at our point in history it is not recognized as a valid way to experience the hidden, veiled, and invisible reality of the feminine. Our culture has lost touch with the mythic dimension of life; we have forgotten how to ground and enrich our lives by interpreting them symbolically. In a television interview, the Protestant theologian Jörg Zink once said that mysticism is, as it were, the inner side of traditional faith. If Christianity does not rediscover its mystical foundations, then it no longer has anything to say. Reflecting on and working with the concept of the Immaculate Conception and the biblical stories has opened an avenue to this dimension for me.

I found that I often needed to take a circular, spiraling pathway in my search to uncover all the possibilities contained in the biblical material. That is not surprising, as the spiral or serpentine force is the very form in which the Goddess's energy manifests. In their book *The Myth of the Goddess,* Baring and Cashford describe the spiral as follows:

> Like the labyrinthine passage through the cave, the spiral and meander symbolize the sacred way to approach to a dimension invisible to human sense.[7]

The Goddess energy, represented by her animal, the serpent, implies our death and rebirth as we approach her. As I reflected on the symbolism of the four women over the years, my interpretation changed and deepened. It shed its "skin" many times over, but its basic structure remained. The spiral moves inward or outward from a center. Movement inward toward the core is always accompanied by the imperative call to sacrifice. We must be prepared to strip away long held beliefs and profoundly question all that we have hitherto placed our faith and trust in or counted on for security. There then arises the possibility of new awareness as we spiral outward, a fortuitous moment in which we are blessed with a newborn light.

In order to familiarize the reader with the way in which I interpret symbolic material, I would like to briefly refer to Joseph Campbell's formulation of the difference between Western and Eastern traditions. He finds that the Eastern, Hindu, and Buddhist traditions place more emphasis on the mystical, while those of the West find significance in historical events. He feels that this is the fundamental problem of discernment between esoteric (mystic) and exoteric (historical) methods of understanding mythic symbols.

I tend to focus more on the esoteric, mystical aspect of symbols and therefore will be using this approach, in the main, to the material I will be examining in the Old Testament. I believe that mystical understanding—which by its very nature includes inspirational and visionary elements—connects us with a transformative divine energy. It has no beginning and no end, it is here and now, yesterday and tomorrow. At the same time, historical events *are* connected linearly in time and space; they do have a beginning and an end, and therefore are more immediately comprehensible to our dualistic, cause-and-effect consciousness, which is an integral part of human existence. I am therefore fully aware of the importance of taking into account the period of presumed time in which the biblical stories occurred. Together, both aspects will bring to light the spiritual principles that sought incarnation in those times. Both aspects, esoteric and exoteric, will reflect a larger and unifying truth.

What does it mean to be a sacred prostitute or a harlot priestess today? It reflects a soul attitude that embraces body and spirit as one and recognizes the sacredness of both dimensions. It is a surrender of our ego power to the mystery of our feminine essence. It is an alignment with divine will through the heart. It is a sacred exposition of our whole being. It is a complete and profound trust in the soul-teacher.

Once, while holding an unknown little boy, I experienced this profound trust in the total surrender of his body in my lap, his soul shining through his eyes as they met mine. Deep inside, I felt our two souls become one. In the words of Jesus: "Whosoever shall not receive the kingdom of God as a little child, shall in no wise enter therein" (Luke 18:17). Restoring trust, surrender, and innocence opens the door to our souls, so that we can perhaps then speak as did the Lady who appeared to the young Bernadette:

> "I am the Immaculate Conception."
> I overcome duality
> So I am free of original sin.
> I am the Alma Mater.

PART ONE

———— ◄O► ————

Mythic Dimensions
of the
Historical Periods
of the Four Women

———— ◄O► ————

THREE OF THE FOUR WOMEN WHO APPEAR in the lineage of Jesus lived in distinct historical periods, each of which had its own character: the story of Tamar takes place in the time of "the Patriarchs," the story of Rahab in the time of "the Judges," and Bathesheba in the time of "the Prophets and Kings." Each of these three major periods can be viewed as a different re-created image of God, mirroring the evolution of the identity of the Hebrew people. In this light, they mark a triple threshold to a new consciousness.

The total epoch encompassing the three periods could be interpreted as an unconscious equivalent or perhaps a mythic prototype of the Christian Trinity, with the Patriarchs representing the Father, the Judges, the Son, and the Kings and Prophets the Holy Ghost. The Book of Ruth, which appears between the time of the Judges and the Prophets and Kings, is autonomous and Ruth is the only one who has her own independent story, in order to transmit a sense out of time, a quality of eternity and at the same time she is a mediatrix between historical time and the eternal mystical aspect of the soul, as you will see in chapter four.

As C. G. Jung observes on this subject: "the Trinity represents the progressive transformation of one and the same substance, namely the psyche as a whole. . . . The rhythm is built up in three steps, but the resultant symbol is a quaternity."[1]

CHRONOLOGICAL TABLE OF EVENTS
IN THE OLD TESTAMENT

The Patriarchs   **2000–1750 BCE**

Tamar   Abraham, Isaac, Jacob,
                                      Joseph
                                      Bronze Age
                                      Genesis 12–50

The Judges   **1220–1020 BCE**

Rahab   Joshua conquers Palestine
                                      Iron Age
                                      The Book of Joshua;
                                      Judges

Between Judges and Prophets

Ruth   The Book of Ruth

The Prophets and Kings   **1020–922 BCE**

Bathsheba   King David
                                      Iron Age
                                      I and II Samuel

ONE

◄◦►

The Patriarchs

The word *patriarch* is defined as "original father." Mircea Eliade informs us that the story of Abraham and the adventures of his son Isaac, his nephews Jacob and Joseph form the period called "the Patriarchs."[1] But today the most accepted chronology is: Abraham, his nephew Lot, his grandson Jacob, and his great-grandson Joseph. At the same time, this by no means implies that Genesis (12–50) is a historical document.[2] Therefore, rather than delving into the historical aspects of this biblical era, I wish to focus on the spiritual principle—the archetype of the father—that evolved during this period.

According to Genesis "God created man in his own image, in the image of God he created him, male and female he created them" (Genesis: 1:27). There are many ways to understand this creation myth. One way is to see it as a reversal of the process by which the Hebrew people created a male God in their own image, reflecting their need for a separate identity as a patriarchal tribe. They had no need to create an image of the Goddess because she was present and powerful at that time. The mythologists Anne Baring and Jules Cashford, writing about the evolution of Yahweh, make the following statement:

A deity that is only a tribal deity reflects the moral values and cultural attitudes of a specific people at a particular historical time—in this case those of Iron Age Hebrews. On the other hand, the image of the divine is transformed as the moral consciousness of a people evolves, and so it is in the Old Testament when the tribal image is challenged through the passion, and often the suffering, of the individual. Mythology in this sense reflects the evolution of consciousness. . . . The history of the evolution of consciousness, reflected in the divine images formulated by all peoples, shows how images of divinity gradually change and evolve over many millennia.[3]

Eliade notes that the religion of the Patriarchs is characterized as the cult of "the god of the father."[4] He goes on to tell us that it manifests itself as "the god of my/your father," as is made evident in Genesis 31:5. The "god of the father" is, in its original sense, the god of the immediate ancestors, whom the sons recognize. In revealing himself to the ancestor, he has attested a sort of kinship. He is a god of nomadic peoples who is not connected to a sanctuary, but to a group of people that he follows and protects.[5]

As they penetrated into the land of Canaan, the Patriarchs were confronted with the cult worship of the god El. Barbara Walker, in her book *The Woman's Encyclopedia of Myths and Secrets*, defines *El* as follows:

General Semitic word or name for a deity, especially in combining forms, as Isra-el, Beth-el, Dani-el, El-ijah. Both El and its plural *elohim*, meaning many deities of both sexes, are the Hebrew words rendered "God" by biblical translators. . . . In Phoenicia, El was the Heavenly Bull at the head of the pantheon, spouse of Asherah as Cow Mother. He usually appeared as a human figure wearing the head or horns of a bull.[6]

Once the god of the Patriarchs became identified with El, he acquired a cosmic dimension, which he would have lacked had he remained a god of clan and family. This is the first historically attested example of a synthesis, in other words an integration, which enriched the cultural patrimony of the Patriarchs.[7]

What is brought to the forefront of our consciousness by the translators and interpreters of the Bible is the male life force: the force that makes laws and war, conquers new lands, calls forth heroes, and makes history. We might call it an exoteric energy. The translators focused on the "original fathers," but the "original mothers" are represented as well.

The wives of the four patriarchs (Abraham, Isaac, Jacob, and Joseph) were Sarah, Rebecca, Leah, and Rachel. These Hebrew matriarchs can be seen as the maternal *Urgrund*—the primordial fundament—the "earth" from which the four foremothers of Jesus arise. The matriarchs are not antagonists of the male principle. They are mythic prefigurations of the process of becoming conscious of the transcendent One. In this process the fourfold feminine life force is united by marriage to its equivalent in the fourfold aspect of the masculine realm.

This union leads to a double quaternary, forming the number eight, a number that symbolizes perfect harmony between the masculine and the feminine and represents an infinite lineage without beginning or end. There is no separation or duality; it is an eternal, timeless lineage in which divisiveness does not exist. The divisiveness takes place exclusively in our minds.

There are some parallels in Greek mysticism. Karl Kerényi points out that in the beginning there was both a primeval Great Goddess in the Demeter mystery cult, who created a double of herself in her daughter and demonstrated the continuity of life in all mothers and daughters, and a primeval Father God in the mysteries of the Kabiri, who evolved further in the special figures of Kabiros, Pais, Pratolaos, and Mitos. As images of the divine, both original divinities are timeless, so in reality they do not represent the beginning, but rather the *Anfangslosigkeit* (beginninglessness) of eternal time; one in a feminine and one in a masculine aspect.

In the biblical stories the male lineage is constricted by man-made laws, with an emphasis on real or presumably real historical events, while the lineage of the mother is not so much a matter of outer name as it is of identity through the soul. This might contribute to the three times four generations, from Abraham to Joseph, the husband of Mary, needed for the principle of Christ as Logos to incarnate in Jesus (Matthew 1:17). The feminine life force was forced beneath the surface, where it lay long buried, yet according to Matthew it took only four women—Tamar, Rahab, Ruth, and Bathsheba—to arrive at Mary, the principle of wisdom (Sophia).

The story of Judah and Tamar, which occurs toward the conclusion of the episodes concerning the Patriarchs, marks the beginning of the lineage of Judah, the fourth son of Jacob. This lineage became one of the most significant in the history of Israel. It also marked the beginning of the "law of the levirate." *Levir* means brother-in-law, and the levirate was the custom by which the brother or next of kin to a deceased man was bound under certain circumstances to marry his widow. This law assured the continuity of life and of patrimony on the male side. This lineage is the polar opposite of the feminine life force embodied by the four biblical women, beginning with Tamar. She marks the first breakthrough, a coming forward of the feminine life force in the lengthy male list in the genealogical tree.

The growing spiritual principle of the father develops in the stories of Abraham, Isaac, Jacob, and Joseph in their search for identity as a nomadic people, and fully incarnates in Judah, the first man who is mentioned in relation to a woman in Matthew's genealogy. As the fourth son of Jacob, he brings to consciousness the latent potential for completion: the original infinite unified energy of female-male become finite. When this energy surfaces in consciousness, it divides and turns into a duality as Tamar and Judah. This might also be interpreted as the mystical, esoteric reason why Judah's lineage became the most significant in Israel's history. It was able to transmit, through spiritual inheritance, the unitary nature of the divine-human, female-male continuum that incarnates in the New Testament as Mary-Jesus.

What does it mean for a woman today to be confronted with the patriarchs on a psychological level? It is not my aim to discuss the concrete historical effects of patriarchal culture on the feminine world, for many outstanding books have already been written on the subject. However, I *can* speak from the experience of its effect on my own life. During my education, I missed a strong father figure. I was forced to move beyond my personal situation, to search deeper on a transpersonal level for the "original fathers." Paradoxically, although my father could not provide a strong father image for me, his very profession as a metallurgical chemist was linked with the world of transformation. Just as the mystic represents the inner side of faith, so the alchemist represents the mystical side of chemistry.

In my personal experience, the "patriarchs" are linked with the beginning of the individuation process and, in my research work, with the "original fathers" of psychology, mythology, and religion, namely C. G. Jung, Joseph Campbell, Erich Neumann, Karl Kerényi, and Mircea Eliade. They helped me to build up background knowledge of the concept of "God as Father" in a positive way. This knowledge became my instrument of differentiation and discrimination. It made it possible for me to take a second step: to find my identity as a woman, my true inner self, my soul. It opened a door and enabled me to enter the world where "God is Mother" and to find my place in the world of the opposites: unknown-known, different-same, lost-found, repressed-redeemed.

In our women's circle, we often discuss the negative psychological effects that the "patriarchs" have on our lives. Surprisingly enough, the disturbing male spirit is transmitted quite frequently through the lineage of the mother. When a mother does not deal with her inner creative male spirit, it develops into an unconscious authority figure. This figure manifests in negative thoughts and judgments, both on a personal level and also on a deeper, traditional Catholic patriarchal level. The effect is one of low self-esteem and a heightened sense of inferiority. There is an overactive participation in the outer world, often in the form of a highly efficient nature in competition with the negative mother. We have a profound need to change the current rhythm of our lives, to move toward the woman who is striving for a fuller development of her inner cyclic rhythm by a listening to the voice of her feminine soul.

It comes down to our own consciousness, to how we individually interpret and experience the concept of God or Goddess—but we need a mirror. In our times we are slowly transforming the patriarchal image of God into a more compassionate, loving, complete image—an image that embraces and contains contrasts and dualities. The more complete we are in ourselves, the more the concept of the divine emerges in its totality. This is reflected in the words of St. Paul:

> For now we see through a glass, darkly; but then face to face: now I know in part; but then shall I know even as also I am known. (I Corinthians 13:12)

TWO

The Judges

The biblical epoch extending from 1200 to 1020 BCE is called the period of the Judges. It begins with Joshua's entry into Canaan and ends with the recognition of Saul's kingship. Eliade describes the Judges as military leaders, counselors, and magistrates.

The verb *to judge* is defined as "the faculty of the human mind to discriminate and pronounce sentence after careful inquiry and deliberation." The number eight card in the Marseilles Tarot deck depicts "Justice," represented as a woman holding an upraised sword in her right hand and a pair of scales in her left. The sword and scales symbolize two different aspects of justice. The upraised sword denotes the rational masculine—the right-hand side—that separates and distinguishes. The sword is vertical and so points upward, toward the spirit. The left-hand side represents the irrational feminine, which balances the dualities in a horizontal line symbolized by the two cups. The scales are being held at heart level, suggesting that balanced justice must include the feelings of the heart. The golden throne upon which Justice resides represents her incorruptibility. This image of Justice represents both divine eternal justice, which maintains the balance of the cosmos, and the centered human being, one able to use the sword and scales as compatible tools on the path to consciousness, tools sensitive to, and in alignment with, the divine will of the soul.

Just as the Judges can be seen as the sons of the original Patriarchs, the emerging spiritual principle incarnating during the period of the Judges is that of the son. In his interpretation of the Trinity, C. G. Jung writes:

"Son" means the transition from a permanent initial stage called "Father" . . . to the stage of being a father oneself. And this means that the son will transmit to his children the procreative spirit of life, which he himself has received and from which he himself was begotten. Brought down to the level of the individual, this symbolism can be interpreted as follows: the state of unreflecting awareness known as "Father" changes into the reflective and rational state of consciousness known as "Son." This state is not only in opposition to the still-existing earlier state, but, by virtue of its conscious and rational nature, it also contains many latent possibilities of dissociation. Increased discrimination begets conflicts that were unconscious before but must now be faced, because, unless they are clearly recognized, no moral decisions can be taken. The stage of the "Son" is therefore a conflict situation. . . .[1]

The Judges section of the Bible is rife with conflicts: wars, conquests and defeats, transgressions, sins, and punishments. It is not surprising that this period is referred to as one of the darkest in the history of Israel. The son represents, in a psychological sense, the power of discrimination seen in Justice's sword. This critical male spirit is often detached from all feeling, which can result in the kind of destruction ordered by Yahweh in the Books of Joshua and Judges:

And they utterly destroyed all that was in the city [Jericho], both man and woman, young and old, and ox, and sheep, and ass, with the edge of the sword. (Joshua 6:21)

And the Lord discomfited them before Israel, and slew them with a great slaughter at Gibeon, and chased them along the way. . . .

And . . . the Lord cast down great stones from heaven upon them
unto Azekah, and they died: they were more which died with hail-
stones than they whom the children of Israel slew with the sword.
(Joshua 10:10–11)

What emerges from these passages is an image of a terrifying god;
a god of war, vengeance, and oppression, a god who is jealous of his
"children" because they are attracted to other gods. This is the male
spirit wielding the killing sword of separation. However, just as the
Hebrew matriarchs balanced the exoteric male life force in the era of
the Patriarchs, in the era of the Judges, a balancing factor appears in
the form of a feminine judge, Deborah.

And Deborah, a prophetess, the wife of Lapidoth, she judged Israel
at that time. And she dwelt under the palm tree of Deborah . . . and
the children of Israel came up to her for judgment. (Judges 4:4–5)

Her presence is important because it points out what is needed in
justice in order to make it whole. Balancing the son, she is the feminine
consciousness seen as daughter, differentiated from the former state of
"mother" or "matriarch." What emerges here is the indestructible feminine life force, symbolized by the Tree of Life where Deborah dwells.
Her decisions as judge and prophetess would have been guided by a
desire to resolve the tensions and conflicts that arose during that period.

Deborah's name also indicates her wider symbolic meaning. In
Hebrew, the name for "bee," *dbure,* comes from the root *dbr,* meaning
"word." Bees and butterflies are ancient images of the soul and linked
with the Goddess of regeneration and transformation. According to the
Women's Encyclopedia of Myths and Secrets, Deborah bears "the same
name as the Goddess incarnate in early Mycenaean and Anatolian
rulers as 'the Pure Mother Bee.'"[2] We could say that Deborah speaks
the language of the soul. She prophesies and judges with soul wisdom.

The conquest of the land of Canaan, which had been promised

to the Patriarchs in divine apparitions (Genesis 12:1–3), might also be understood as signifying the repression and ultimate destruction of a matriarchal culture. But—along with the presence of Deborah—the story of Rahab, woven into the tale of the destruction of Jericho, makes it clear that the Goddess survived. We read that Rahab's "house was upon the town wall, and she dwelt upon the wall" (Joshua 2:15). As we will explore in more depth in chapter five, Jericho itself is a symbol for the Great Mother, which indicates a matriarchal structure and order in the psyche in which the Goddess is the dominant archetype. The Hebrew invaders, wielding the sword of discrimination, represent the assertion of external order. This male force was not in relation with the female force and so it ended in the total destruction of Jericho.

Rahab is on the threshold, straddling the wall between outer and inner space, while overlooking both sides. This suggests that in the process of redeeming the Goddess's spiritual memory, we must constantly keep our glance directed at, and take into consideration, both inner and outer reality, both the masculine and the feminine. Such a task entails maintaining our balance on the threshold at the midpoint between the two worlds. For from this vantage point, we are able to recognize and unite polarities.

Rahab hides two spies who come on behalf of the invading conqueror, Joshua, in return for their assurance of safety for herself and her family. But her actions are not the betrayal they may appear to be, because they serve to save the values of a matriarchal culture (through Achan), which would otherwise have been destroyed. After saving the lives of the two spies, she tells them:

> Get you to the mountain, lest the pursuers meet you; and hide your-
> selves there three days, until the pursuers be returned: and after-
> ward may ye go your way. (Joshua: 2:16)

Going to the mountain represents an ascent to a higher plane. The mountain symbolizes a connection between earth and sky, between the human and the divine. It is the task of priests, angels, explorers, messengers, sacred prostitutes, and visionaries to be the thread that connects these opposites. They are mediators between the polarities. The three days in hiding represents sustaining a state of tension until a third thing emerges from the unconscious as the unifying aspect of love.

In Kerényi's discussion of the two timeless lineages of the divine in Greek mysticism, one masculine and one feminine, he introduces a third aspect, which is more psychic than male or female. This is represented by Eros, or love. The priestess Diotima, in Plato's *Symposium*, explains that Eros is neither god nor human. He is in between the divine and the mortal. Since he stands at midpoint between the two, he is true to both, so that the whole is conjoined in itself.

In the Bible, this third aspect of an eternal line without beginning or end is represented by the angels. Angels are invisible and winged, like Eros. They are messengers between gods and goddesses and human beings. They nurture with infinite love, compassion, and never-ending patience, and in so doing, help the human to merge with the divine. They bring us back home, back to our place of origin. So it is not surprising that an angel appears in the story of Joshua to guide his conquest of the Promised Land. The story of their encounter, which we will explore in more detail in chapter five, also guides Joshua's movement toward a more encompassing understanding.

From a psychological standpoint, the conquest of the Promised Land can be viewed as a process of penetration into the unconscious. Although such research into our soul gives meaning to our lives, it is always a challenge, for it involves victories and defeats, death and rebirth. We see this reflected in the dreams and visions of our soul landscapes. In this sense, the conquest of the Promised Land also symbolizes the broadening of the horizons of consciousness that takes place when a new aspect of the unconscious is brought to light and integrated into consciousness.

For a certain period of my life, I was afforded the opportunity to meet regularly with a group of Jungian analysts. This became my personal experience of the Judges. These analysts were all spiritual sons and daughters of C. G. Jung. As the only nonprofessional in the group, I was challenged and given the chance to measure and compare my reactions and knowledge with theirs. At that time I lacked the courage to present my own work, fearing I could not bear their judgment. With time, however, my critical capacities strengthened. I began to develop my own opinions. I became aware of the areas of agreement as well as those of disagreement. In so doing, I reinforced my own self-worth, slowly acknowledging my own inner judge and taking another personal step in the evolution of my own consciousness.

This group had been brought together by Marie-Louise von Franz, a spiritual daughter of Jung's. She wanted to experiment with an assembly of analysts who would function in a group setting that did not have an organized structure. Von Franz used the image of bees to describe the way that individuals could work in harmonious cooperation without a rational organization. She states that such groups existed in Zen Buddhism and mystery cults, which were "gripped by the same living symbol; they were strong, social bodies, which functioned without too many outer regulations." At Eleusis and Ephesus, the mystics were called "bees."

I had a mystical experience of my own with bees. One summer day I was sitting quietly in my garden, when my attention was drawn to a bee gathering nectar from a lavender blossom. Suddenly, there was a shift in my awareness. I became one with the bee, I experienced an indescribable sense of oneness not only with the bee, but also with the whole universe. I felt the interconnectedness of life. My eyes absorbed the colors of nature with an almost painful intensity. Everything was more luminous. It was as though I were experiencing the reality behind the veil of illusion. I felt blessed to have felt all this through the eyes of a humble bee—or was I seeing through the eyes of the Goddess?

There is another aspect in the rich symbolism of the bee upon which I would like to focus:

Bees, like all insects that spin cocoons or weave webs, serve as images of the miraculous interconnectedness of life. The intricate cellular structure that secretes the golden essence of life is an image of the network of invisible nature that relates all things to each other in an ordered harmonious pattern.[3]

Feminine consciousness is based on this instinctual awareness of the interconnectedness of life. We see this when comparing it with the male power of discrimination, which implies an attitude of either/or: *either* masculine *or* feminine, dark *or* light. The "bringing into balance" symbolized by the scales of Justice speaks of both/and: the masculine *and* the feminine, the inclusion of the dualities in a balanced, harmonious way.

Considering the many injustices, the abuses of human rights and those of nature, and the wars and conflicts that rage in our own historical period, we must concede that we are still in a state of the sons. This state is a result of a predominately one-sided rational, male-oriented consciousness. When focusing our attention on the reality of evil, injustice, and ferocity, it is difficult to maintain faith in and hope for a better world. Currently, however, there are many signs of a slow but constantly expanding feminine consciousness, weaving an invisible and visible web on a cosmic level. Many men and women are contributing their efforts to bring to consciousness our need to relate and connect, to bring our world once more into harmony, to make this invisible truth of the soul visible.

While reflecting on this chapter, I had a dream about the inevitability of the confrontation with evil, with the devil, in life. The dream spoke of not dwelling in evil, as I had been tempted to do. A wise man once said to me "Mind your words. If you speak of evil, you can get crushed. If you speak of darkness, you become dark. Your substance is the light." The I Ching makes the same point in Hexagram 11: *Tai*— Peace, which emphasizes that the best way to fight evil is to make vigorous progress in the good. The Bible similarly states "resist not evil" (Matthew 5:39).

How many of the conflicts and wars both within us and without could be avoided if we would only trust in and be guided by the science of love?

> The science of love is the science of unity
> Where divisions are harmonies of the eternal,
> Infinite harmony.

THREE

Prophets and Kings

The Book of Judges closes with the following line:

> In those days there was no king in Israel: every man did that which
> was right in his own eyes. (Judges 21:25)

These words express the need to search for a new image, in this
case a king, who could reestablish order in a chaotic world. Kings symbolize the dominant collective consciousness; they represent the divine
principle in visible form. Kings and Prophets could be understood as
an answer to the conflicts constellated in the period of the Judges and,
as such, would symbolize the next step.

Mircea Eliade calls this period of time (1010–970 BCE) the height
of syncretism, which is defined as "arbitrary conciliation between philosophical and religious doctrines, which are basically incompatible."
Syncretism reached a proportion till then unknown, since the monarchy encouraged the fusion of ideas and religious practices shared by the
two stratums of the population, Israelite and Canaanite. King Solomon
accepted the cults of his foreign spouses and permitted them the edifi-
cation of sanctuaries in honor of their gods and goddesses.

Turning to the First Book of Samuel, we encounter, at the outset, a
woman who, in her suffering, challenges the image of the divine in the

period of the Judges. She is Hannah, one of the two wives of Elkanah, who was barren.

> And when the time was that Elkanah offered, he gave to Peninniah,
> his wife and to all her sons and daughters, portions;
> But unto Hannah he gave a worthy portion, for he loved Hannah:
> but the Lord had shut up her womb. (I Samuel 1:4–5)

Here "the Lord" represents the collective consciousness of that time, which was responsible for her infertility: the time was neither open nor ripe for a transformation of the divine image. Hannah's suffering is described as follows:

> And she was in bitterness of soul, and prayed unto the Lord, and
> wept sore. . . . I am a woman of sorrowful spirit: I . . . have poured
> out my soul before the Lord. (I Samuel 1:10, 15)

The woman Hannah, grieving over her childlessness, is a symbol of the soul in search of a new image of the divine, a new fertility.

> childlessness testifies that the connection with the creative earth of
> the psyche has been broken and that a gulf lies between the values
> and ideas of collective consciousness and the dark, fertile loam of
> unconscious, archetypal processes of transformation.[1]

Only the suffering, grieving, and loving soul can bridge the abyss by divine grace, a soul that is ready to sacrifice the thing most desired. In Hannah's case, the thing she most desired was a son; in praying for him she says:

> O Lord of hosts, if thou . . . wilt give unto thine handmaid a man
> child, then I will give him unto the Lord all the days of his life. (I
> Samuel 1:11)

It is often noted in the literature that she is the first woman to initiate conversation with God.[2] Her son Samuel, promised to the Lord by his mother—in an act of conscious service to a higher power—symbolizes a new consciousness committed to a higher purpose. This developed and balanced consciousness is able to bridge the transition from the period of Judges to that of Kings, and to initiate the connection with the third element in the Christian Trinity, that of the Holy Spirit. Samuel was the last of the Judges:

> And Samuel judged Israel all the days of his life. (I Samuel 7:15)

He is also a prophet, who, like all prophets and prophetesses, foretells and foresees events by divine inspiration. Jungian psychologist Helen Luke explains this in the following manner:

> [I]n those days a prophet was a person capable of ecstasy, of being filled with the spirit. The prophet was the "seer," or, as we would now say, one in whom the deep unconscious has been activated and to whom is given the choice between meeting and relating to the powers thus released or succumbing to possession by them.[3]

However, it is extremely difficult to make the transition from the "state of the son" to that of "the Holy Spirit," as we see in Samuel's sons:

> And his sons walked not in his ways . . . and perverted judgment. Then all the elders . . . came to Samuel. . . .
> And said unto him . . . thy sons walk not in thy ways: now make us a king to judge us like all the nations. (I Samuel 8:3–5)

The tragic story of Saul, the prophet and first king, reflects the danger inherent in the transition from the old to the new image of the divine. Helen Luke, in her essay on the story of Saul, defines a prophet as "a person burning with the strength and beauty of an inner vision, a channel for the wisdom of God, but one who nevertheless remains human, related to this gift of the spirit and never identified with it."[4] She makes it clear that "The gift of the Spirit is a capacity for vision. It can carry us to wholeness if we accept the price, or it can consume and destroy our humanity."[5]

> But, one who allows ecstasy to remain on the emotional level, who loses his or her ordinary humanity or is incapable of the kind of obedience that the inner voice demands, will be split and destroyed by the "gift of the spirit" and will end up in the clutches of the demonic side of it, as did Saul.[6]

The commitment needed to the inner voice is one of sacrifice and constant vigilance, which is symbolically represented by the act of anointment. Oil and ointments represent the life substance of the soul in its innermost condition of spiritual surrender. The following text illustrates Saul's inability to honor the gift of spirit:

> Then Samuel took the horn of oil and anointed him [David], in the midst of his brethren: and the Spirit of the Lord came upon David from that day forward. . . .
> But the Spirit of the Lord departed from Saul, and an evil spirit from the Lord troubled him. (I Samuel 16:13–14)

The spirit departed from Saul because he used it for his personal power and did not listen to his inner voice. Samuel, as judge, prophet, and priest, holds the solution to this danger. He is capable of reflection, compassion, and discrimination in the process of encountering the power of the unconscious while maintaining a stable ego.

> Just as the transition from the first stage to the second demands the sacrifice of childish dependence, so, at the transition to the third stage, an exclusive independence has to be relinquished.[7]

Samuel represents our ability to subordinate our ego consciousness, our exclusive independence, to a superior totality; to serve it, to follow the inner voice unconditionally. Throughout the whole story of Israel's monarchy, there is always a prophet at the side of the king to remind him that a king is merely a servant of Yahweh (David and Nathan are one example). In consequence, the totality of the psyche becomes effective, which is realized in spiritual motherhood and fatherhood.

The Book of Kings might represent the principle of order, centeredness, and the predominant consciousness of that time. The figure of David as the second king reflects a type of activity overly involved in outer events and riddled with conflicts similar to those that beset Saul, who was seized by inner forces. In Jungian terms we would call them extroverted and introverted attitudes. This triggered a conflict between two unbalanced aspects, as represented in Saul's jealousy of David and his attempt on David's life.

David makes his own missteps as a result of his ego-thrust:

And it came to pass, after the year was expired, at the time when kings go forth to battle, that David sent Joab, and his servants with him, and all Israel and they destroyed the children of Ammon, and besieged Rabbah. But David tarried still at Jerusalem.

And it came to pass in an eveningtide, that David arose from off his bed, and walked upon the roof of the king's house: and from the roof he saw a woman washing herself; and the woman was very beautiful to look upon.

And David sent and inquired after the woman. And one said, Is this not Bathsheba, the daughter of Eliam, the wife of Uriah the Hittite?

And David sent messengers, and took her; and she came in unto him, and he lay with her; for she was purified from her uncleanness: and she returned unto her house.

And the woman conceived, and sent and told David, and said, I am with child. (II Samuel 11:1–5)

David's reaction is far from laudable. First, he calls Uriah home from the wars, hoping that he will sleep with his wife so the baby will appear to be his. Then, when Uriah's sense of duty as a warrior interferes, David orders him to the front lines and certain death. He is cursed for these actions in Nathan's prophecy:

> Now therefore the sword shall never depart from thine house; because thou hast despised me, and has taken the wife of Uriah the Hittite to be thy wife. (II Samuel 12:10)

Although David and Bathsheba's first son dies, their second son is Solomon, who plays a major role in the history of Israel. Despite his fame, wisdom, and glory as a rich and powerful king, he seems to have faltered as well:

> And he had seven hundred wives, princesses, and three hundred concubines: and his wives turned away his heart. . . .
> Solomon did evil in the sight of the Lord. . . .
> And the Lord was angry with Solomon. . . . (I Kings 11:3,6,9)

Solomon's kingdom was split and he was unable to unite it in peace, so it was partitioned after his death. The two resultant kingdoms, the one of Israel and the other of Judah, were constantly and with terrible cruelty at war with each other. The situation described recalls a similar one in the Book of Judges; as such, we recognize it as a regression, as a failure to create a new image of the divine.

These examples evoke many parallels from our own time, when a new consciousness is slowly emerging. Inevitably, we have an accompanying inflation of prophets and prophecies. There is a profound yearning in our souls to be in touch with the divine and to be filled with spirit, be it through books, charismatic leaders, sweeping social movements, or religion. The young people who take the drug "ecstasy" at discos are reflecting this longing in their own way.

Now, as then, what is needed is the ability to discriminate with the mind *and* the heart. The ability to do this seems to hinge on the need to make a deeper, even an absolute commitment, to surrender to the inner voice in complete trust and love. As we have seen in the story of Saul, the Holy Spirit and its gifts are symbolized by holy oil. To listen to our inner voice is to anoint it, that is, to nurture it and further the life of our relationship with it. In the individual, it is reflected in the daily discipline of prayer, meditation, and paying attention to dreams and visions and synchronous events.

In my personal life, I encountered the "Prophets" for the first time as an inner voice telling me to search for the meaning of the Immaculate Conception. This voice was a strong instinct, urging me down the path with great determination. Initially I succumbed many times to possession by unconscious powers and was incapable of relating to them on a conscious level. But after many abortive attempts, the inner voice became more distinct and my resolve deepened. These processes, of succumbing to possession, becoming inflated, and making abortive attempts are all part of being human. Going through these experiences is an important step toward consciousness. Although I have also been sidetracked by false prophets, a healthy instinct set me back on my own path.

The inner voice can also come from without. In my case, it came through a clairvoyant friend who ordered me to do what I feared most: travel to an old Mayan ruin in the middle of the jungle. This became a heroine's quest—though I did not feel remotely heroic, but rather vulnerable, ill, and quite terrified. At the same time, I did not realize that my main task was to develop my ability to heed the inner voice and to learn to discriminate between false voices and those that speak from the core. My two friends and I promptly fell into the trap of following a false voice, with the result that we found ourselves in dangerous, even life-threatening situations. The name of the voice ordering us on this journey was "Mercedes," a Spanish word meaning "grace." In Italian, the word *mercede* means "the reward given for putting oneself in the service of love," synonymous with "courtesy," "grazie," "merci."

What I thought was the end of our outer difficult pilgrimage was only an initiation of the soul's journey into the underworld. I was taken to my limits: limits experienced as a death of my old self, beyond which I felt only a black, limitless hole. Jung states that "The decisive question for man is: Is he related to something infinite or not? This is the telling question of his life."[8] This question became the focus of my life. In time, my inner voice became more definite and clear, taking the form of an angel called Emannuel, which means "God is with you." To this "male" spirit was added a "female," Sophia. In this way, the infinite became personified. I have no doubt that this is a manifestation of the spirit of love, the comforter who has been promised to humankind, "that he may abide with you forever" (John 14:16).

Von Franz points out that from the very beginnings of Christianity, the Holy Spirit has represented an embarrassing aspect of God's image, because it can enter directly into the individual. She remarks that if we consider the three aspects of the Trinity as distinct—which is inexact, because they are also one person—the Holy Spirit is the only one of the three with whom the Christian can communicate in every moment. God the Father never descended to earth, and Christ, after his resurrection, ascended to heaven, but the Holy Spirit can descend repeatedly into every human being without any restrictions on time and space.

The spirit of truth defies any definition according to gender. It can be called "Ruach," "Spirit of God," "Holy Spirit," "Logos," "Sophia," or "Comforter." It lends us the grace to experience the divine as a feminine or masculine manifestation or to simultaneously transcend them both in a union of opposites. This concept relates to the three limitless lines in Greek mysticism. As we have seen, the third line is neither male nor female but stands at the midpoint between the two, serving both, so that the whole is brought together.

FOUR

◄◦►

The Feminine Divine
and the
Reclaiming of Wholeness

The Christian Trinity symbolizes an evolution of male consciousness in relation to the image of a male God, which excludes the feminine and, as such, is incomplete. Although the feminine divine was active in the time of the Patriarchs, Judges, and Prophets, it was not truly incorporated. In the time of the Kings, the image of the Goddess was not personified in a queen, but rather split off. There was an attempt in Bathsheba, but it failed because the soul-giving life force of love was missing. A union of opposites, a sacred union, was not possible, so a purely arbitrary one occurred.

Yet running beneath all this like a silent current in a stream is the limitless life force that emerges time and again. We can see it particularly in the recurring presence of Hannah, the goddess of a thousand faces. From the mother of Samuel, to Hannah, the grandmother of Jesus in an apocryphal legend, to Hannah as crone and prophetess who receives the Jesus child at the temple (Luke: 2:25–38), she is the thread guiding us through the labyrinth of the biblical stories. Hannah in Greek is Anna, signifying "grace." In Sanskrit it translates as "cosmic vital essence." Hannah is also St. Anne, whom Barbara Walker describes as:

Mythical mother of the Virgin Mary from the Middle-Eastern Goddess Anna, or Hannah or Di-Ana, mother of Mari. From Sumeria to pre-Roman Latium, she was known as Anna, the Grandmother-Goddess; Anatha in Syria, Anat in Canaan, Ana or Anah in several Old Testament transformations. Long before the Bible was written, the Goddess Anna was already known as the Grandmother of the God. . . .

Romans worshipped her as the Goddess Anna Perenna, "Eternal Anna," mother of the Aeons. She stood at the change of the years, a two-headed Goddess of Time with two faces named Prorsa and Postverta, looking forward and backward from her heavenly gate among the stars, where one celestial cycle merged into the next. So she stood for both Alpha and Omega. . . .[1]

Despite the repression of the Goddess in the Old Testament, the image of the female paralleled the evolution of the male image as a shadow. It is interesting to note that the evolution of the male images gave structure to the female shadow. We can see this on an individual inner level as well. The clearer the male spirit becomes, the more we are able to recognize our rejected female side on a personal as well as a cultural level. If we can accept the images of the patriarchs, judges, prophets, and kings as a necessary evolution of male consciousness in man *and* in woman rather than a depreciation of the feminine, we discover that the corresponding hidden matriarchs, female judges, prophetesses, and queens are equally valid archetypal images of the evolution of the divine. As we are told by quantum physics, reality is dependent upon the observer.

On a psychological level, the Christian Trinity teaches us that as long as we hold male and female to be opposites, superior or inferior, we remain stuck, in our development, at the second level, the one Jung calls "the stage of the son," the state of conflict that we have identified with the period of the Judges in the Bible. We need to find a middle avenue, an avenue of love, of Holy Spirit, of wisdom, where both sides are honored as equal. On a psychological level, it is a question of harmony.

In the biblical Genesis, love is represented by the cherubim that guard the Tree of Life. The flaming sword in this context is a metaphor for the capacity to transform, through fire, the life experience into wisdom; it is analogous to the alchemical process of death and rebirth. In the thirteenth century *Die Legenda Aurea* (*The Golden Legend or Lives of the Saints*), cherubim express the completeness of knowledge; for this reason they are called "the abundance of wisdom." The masculine and feminine life forces need the third aspect of love to become whole, to become one, to "get married," as we will see in the story of Ruth. Her story reveals that the realm of the middle is situated in the human soul as the missing fourth, as part of the divine. The soul is the only place where the divine third can become whole.

> The rhythm is built up in three steps, but the resultant symbol is a quaternity. . . . In Pythagoras the great role was played not by three but by four; the Pythagorean oath, for instance, says that "the tetraktys contains the roots of eternal nature" . . . [and] the Pythagorean school was dominated by the idea that the soul was a square. . . .[2]

Or, as expressed in the famous alchemical saying of Maria Prophetissa: "One becomes two, two becomes three, and out of the third comes the one as the fourth."

This axiom is trying to describe a mysterious transformation that transpires within the soul in a realm beyond the reach of words. What is needed is total surrender to the divine present in our souls and present in our humble daily lives, which are both the most difficult and the easiest of all tasks. Ruth's story teaches us that the experience of our divine wholeness is the experience of returning home through the transformation of the flaming sword to the Tree of Life, our divine source and roots.

PART TWO

The Stories of Tamar, Rahab, Ruth, and Bathsheba

A Symbolic Interpretation

FIVE

Tamar

The Sacred Prostitute

She is a tree of life to them that lay hold upon her;
and happy is every one that retaineth her.

PROVERBS 3:18

The story of Tamar told in Genesis 38 suggests and expresses a powerful indestructible divine feminine energy that personifies in a mythic way. Tamar herself represents an archetype of divine feminine power, revealed by her name, which translates as "palm tree."

> In the Babylonian myth of the primal garden, the palm tree was the Tree of Life, a dwelling-place of the Goddess Astarte. The Hebrew version of her name was Tamar, "Palm Tree."[1]

It is significant that Tamar is the first woman mentioned in the genealogical tree of Jesus, which is also a symbolic Tree of Life. As such, Tamar captures our attention as the soul-foremother of Jesus. Symbolically speaking, she represents Jesus's feminine divine roots. Jung states in *Mysterium Coniunctionis*: "According to the Koran, Sura 19,

Mary was born under a palm tree, just as Leto gave birth under a palm tree in Delos."[2] In the wisdom literature of the Bible, Sophia relates:

> I was exalted like a palm tree in En-gaddi,
> and as a rose plant in Jericho,
> as a fair olive in a pleasant field,
> and grew up as a plane tree by the water.
> (Ben Sirach 24:14)

The Tree of Life is a universal symbol of the matter from which eternal life springs. The Greeks considered the palm tree a tree of light and dedicated it to both Helios and Apollo. The Greek name for palm is *phoenix,* indicating its close symbolic proximity to the mystical bird of immortality. Jung sees, in the palm's upward rising form, a symbol of the soul, and in the tree itself, a symbol of the process of individuation. In this sense, the story of Tamar marks the beginning of the evolution of the human soul.

The Tree of Life was one of the primary images of the goddess herself, in whose immanent presence all pairs of opposites are reconciled. Growing on the surface of the earth, with roots below and branches above, the tree was the great pillar that united earth with heaven and the underworld, through which the energies of the cosmos poured continually into earthly creation. The animating spirit that moved within it was the serpent, guardian also of the fruit or treasure of the tree, which was the epiphany of the goddess, that is, the *experience* of unity.[3]

In the Old Testament, in Genesis, the eating of the fruit from the Tree of Knowledge brought about the *loss* of the experience of unity. Today we are experiencing that loss in the extreme: the Goddess is not only denied a presence in our souls, but also in nature. This becomes obvious when we view the ongoing destruction of our planet. The continual decimation of the rain forests, which constitute the lungs of our planet, is an alarming sign that we are destroying ourselves along with Mother Earth. It is an inevitable consequence of the loss of the fruit of the Tree of Life, of the *felt* or *experienced* unity of matter and spirit.

As mentioned earlier, the archetypal soul form representing the vehicle of relationship with the Goddess was called the "sacred prostitute or harlot priestess": a psychic structure that was integrated into the religious life of the culture of ancient times.

> Inanna and Ishtar were the goddesses of sexual love and fertility and one of their titles was "Hierodule of Heaven." *Hierodule* is a Greek word that means "sacred work" or "servant of the holy." The word "harlot" or "prostitute," which is often used to describe the priestesses of Inanna and Ishtar, no longer conveys the original sacredness of their service to the goddess, although the original meaning of the word "prostitute" was "to stand on behalf of." The priestesses who served in the temple of Inanna or Ishtar were the vehicles of her creative life in their sexual union with the men who came there to perform a sacred ritual.[4]

The role of the sacred prostitute prior to and during biblical times was to take the place of the Goddess, in whom sexual and spiritual natures were one. A Goddess who embraces both the physical and psychical aspects of matter unites sexual pleasure with spirituality. A beautiful example of this union is the erotically spiritual "Song of Solomon" in the Old Testament. The sacred prostitute embodies the capacity to relate to the divine as a whole through love. In many biblical interpretations, however, Tamar is viewed as a disguised harlot and is morally stigmatized through the assignment of a literal meaning to the role she plays in the story of Judah and his sons, told in Genesis 38. She is called a deceiver, a cheat, and a sinner.

Even though Tamar was married to Er, Judah's firstborn son, he was not able to relate to her in a fruitful way, because he "was wicked in the sight of the Lord; and the Lord slew him" (Genesis 38:7). So in order to fulfill the law of the levirate, Judah told his second son, Onan, to marry her.

> And Onan knew that the seed should not be his; and it came to pass that he spilled it on the ground. . . .
>   And the thing which he did displeased the Lord: wherefore he slew him also. (Genesis 38:9, 10)

The sons of Judah incorporate a male energy unable to relate consciously and creatively to a powerful Goddess, so they waste the divine seed. Not honoring the divine—in this case, the Goddess—constellates her destructive aspect. Owing to the behavior of the sons of Judah, Tamar becomes a widow. The ancient etymological root of the word *widow* is "bereaved, separated, divided." The divine feminine is separated from consciousness, which could be considered the underlying reason for sterility. Judah, afraid that his third son will also die, makes an intriguing request of Tamar:

> Remain a widow at thy father's house, till Shelah my son be grown. . . .
>   And Tamar went and dwelt in her father's house. (Genesis 38:11)

There are several ways of interpreting this quotation. At that time, a woman was owned in the first place by her father and only in the second place by her husband. In a less literal context, Tamar would represent the personal feminine soul that is imprisoned in patriarchal consciousness, represented by the father's house. She is in mourning as "one who is separated," a widow.

It seems strange that the period of the Patriarchs should call forth a sacred prostitute. But since the Hebrew people could not possibly ignore the powerful presence of the Goddess, Tamar's story suggests that she could also be interpreted as the development of the feminine principle. This development, which leads away from the primordial connection to the mother and toward consciousness, transpires largely through the masculine self, which plays a redeeming role for the feminine principle—whether it be experienced transpersonally or personally, inwardly or outwardly.[5]

The other, masculine "self" is represented in this case by the two sons of Judah, Judah himself, and Tamar's father. "Dwelling at the father's house" could be interpreted positively, as a fruitful time of withdrawal from the outer world. It also reflects the sense of distance we, as women, feel from the maternal Garden of Eden. From a feminine standpoint we are "widows" because we are in a state of separation and are no longer identified unconsciously with the mother. In this situation, we have to relate to our other, masculine "self." As Tamar's story tells us, this relationship begins on a personal level. Building up a consciousness grounded in the positive value and thoughts of the "Patriarchs," the archetype of the father can give us the ability to redeem and integrate our sacred prostitute nature.

Tamar, as one face of the fourfold self, as goddess of love, sexuality, and fertility, seeks to incarnate in all our relationships. Every love relationship begins with an experience of identification with the divine (the condition of being in the Garden of Eden). This is followed by transgression (the serpent, the fall into duality) in the form of sinking into matter (Eve). Then there is the process of incarnation, which contains both masculine and feminine (Eve-Adam). To attain to a manifest spiritual experience on earth (Mary-Christ), it is necessary to go through a process of coming to consciousness, that is, of coming to an understanding of the polarities of feminine and masculine. This happens through the meeting or clash of these energies, which in their different forms are in search of an earthly and cosmic synthesis.

In this sense, Tamar initiates a process of soul consciousness, which is not rejected by the masculine—in this case, Judah. First, Judah became a widower himself, a state that indicates a loss of relatedness to the feminine.

And in process of time the daughter of Shuah Judah's wife died; and Judah was comforted, and went up unto his sheep shearers to Timnath, he and his friend Hirah, the Adullamite. (Genesis 38:12)

Tamar was informed that her father-in-law was coming up to Timnath to shear his sheep:

And she put her widow's garments off from her, and covered her with a veil, and wrapped herself, and sat in an open space, which is by the way to Timnath; for she saw that Shelah was grown, and she was not given unto him to wife. (Genesis 38:14)

Another version (*La Sacra Bibbia*) tells us that Tamar covered her face with a veil and perfumed herself and sat by the door of Enajim (Genesis 38:14). Perfume is a feminine instrument of attraction behind which lies the hidden call of the weightless fragrance of the soul. It is like an invisible embrace. The door of Enajim might be understood as a place of transition between two worlds or two sources: the known and the unknown, the feminine and the masculine. The door opens onto a mystery. Tamar is the door leading to a deeper comprehension and experience of love and relationship expressed in the sexual act. It is the most direct physical avenue to divine manifestation, and as such should be kept secret and veiled.

The *Dictionnaire des Symboles* defines a veil as that which separates two things: depending upon whether you put it on or take it off, it signifies either a hidden awareness or a revelation. Tamar is both widow and sacred prostitute, both hidden awareness and revelation, for after meeting Judah she "laid by her veil from her, and put on the garment of her widowhood" (Genesis 38:19).

The motif of the veil comes into all religions. You could say that the deepest experiences have to be kept secret and do by nature remain secret, and it would be most destructive to face them oneself or to tell anyone else.[6]

There are secret things of the soul that can only grow in the dark—the clear sun of consciousness burns the life away.[7]

This may be the reason why, after meeting Judah, Tamar donned the garments of widowhood. And this could also be the reason why Judah, representing masculine consciousness, did not recognize Tamar.

Most interpretations reduce Tamar to a disguised harlot whom Judah failed to recognize as such. However, there are other, less reductive ways to examine this story. "The changing of clothes in the mysteries stood for transformation into an enlightened understanding,"[8] explains von Franz. Tamar was not disguising herself as a prostitute but rather was revealing her true nature. She was transmitting the truth on behalf of the divine to humankind. The Goddess thus reveals herself here as the sacred prostitute.

In my personal life, I met Tamar when I discovered the power contained in a woman's body through her sexuality. I learned also that we do not own this power. It is the "servant of the Holy" and stands on behalf of it. I believe that this is the deepest meaning of the term "sacred prostitute." Man's primal unconscious fear of woman originated in woman's sexual power. The image of a purified virgin, free from sexuality that we find in the Catholic Church, reflects this fear.

Men and women both are often victims and not instigators in love. Tamar becomes a woman who shows the way—a teacher of the responsibility women carry in a love relationship. At the risk of her own life, she behaves uninhibitedly in order to make a relationship fruitful and, at the same time, to stay true to her innermost self.

As he turned into her by the way, and said . . . I pray thee, let me come in unto thee. . . . And she said, what wilt thou give me, that thou mayest come in unto me?

And he said, I will send thee a kid from the flock. And she said, Wilt thou give me a pledge, till thou send it?

And he said, what pledge shall I give thee? And she said, Thy signet, and thy bracelets, and thy staff that is in thine hand. And he gave it to her, and came in unto her, and she conceived by him.

And she arose, and went away, and laid by her veil from her, and put on the garments of her widowhood. (Genesis 38:16–19)

When we meet our sacred prostitute, nature demands a commitment, an active involvement, and a binding promise to be related to the goddess of love, to be a servant of the Holy. The goal is not marriage but fruitfulness of the soul. The many divorces and difficulties in relationships occur when we do not recognize the sacred divine dimensions in every love relationship. Not infrequently, a couple's physical sterility is a sign that they need to make the relationship fruitful on a spiritual level. We are not prepared to give and receive love without attaching conditions. Tamar asked Judah to offer something in trade in exchange for the divine gift of herself. Historically, the exchange of goods at this time was typically in the form of livestock, utensils, and seeds. Judah promised Tamar a kid from the flock.

The promised gift of the kid symbolizes the sacrifice we have to offer up to the Goddess. The association of the goat with a manifestation of the divine is very ancient. In many traditions, the goat appears as a symbol of a nurse and initiatrix in both a physical and mystical sense. Tamar is an initiatrix and nurse of the Goddess mysteries on both the physical and psychic levels.

The story is reminding us that before being initiated into the mysteries of the Goddess, we are asked to make a pledge, which is symbolized by Judah's signet, bracelets, and staff. To make a pledge binding, we must provide proof of our sincerity in the form of a valued object, just as a borrower must offer something of concrete worth as security for his debt to the loaner, who in this instance is Tamar.

The three pledges represent qualities of male energy in the person of Judah. These energies are psychological instruments of discernment, which need to be recognized and integrated at the beginning of an evolutionary process. They partake of the divine and hence endow the recipient or holder with divine power. To express it in more personal terms, I can attest that without these male forces, I would not be writing this book with such rock-solid commitment and the unshakable knowledge that this is my path, my life task that I must accomplish, whatever the outcome may be.

In Tamar's story, the three pledges later redeemed her life. This masculine power of redeeming consciousness is often experienced in projected form. A woman is endangered if the man upon whom she has projected her need for redemption is "charged" with divine power. We can see this in the example of blind attachments to a guru. In personal relationships, this creates a state of dangerous confusion because there is no discrimination, and it can result in an identification of the male partner with the savior archetype. Tamar does not keep the pledges; in the end, she gives them back to their rightful owner, Judah.

In the ancient Orient, seals represented ownership as well as the power of personality. In the Bible, seals belong to God, since divine mysteries are "sealed." This suggests that symbolically speaking, the male power in Judah was divine and belonged to God. The chains and bracelets have the same symbolic meaning as the cord: the union between heaven and earth, and the capacity to be committed and related to both the inner and outer and the masculine and feminine in a fruitful, fertile way.

In *The Interpretation of Fairy Tales,* von Franz explains the symbolism of the staff as follows:

> The staff is a sign of power and judgment, two royal prerogatives symbolized by the king's scepter. The staff is also associated with the Way and is a direction-giving principle in the unconscious. The bishop's staff, for instance, was interpreted by the church as the authority of the doctrine, which shows the way and gives decisions. . . . In antiquity, the golden staff or magic rod belonged to Mercurius and represents his ability to marshal intractable elements within the unconscious. If one has a staff, one is not wholly passive; one has a direction.[9]

To summarize the symbolic meaning of the pledges in our story, we could say that a deep, mysterious and balanced exchange takes place between divine feminine and masculine power; this exchange is not controlled by the conscious mind and is experienced as a blessing and a grace. The soul conceives—and this conception might be a book, or a new project, or a new consciousness.

> And Judah sent the kid by the hand of his friend the Adullamite, to receive his pledge from the woman's hand: but he found her not.
>
> Then he asked the men of that place, saying, Where is the harlot, that was openly by the way side? And they said, there was no harlot in this place. (Genesis 38:20–21)

Why could Hirah not find her? The answer is that Judah alone was able to see her because she was as a personal divine revelation, a hidden awareness. It was a soul experience, and hence one not visible to the outer world. But Judah had not yet recognized who Tamar really was.

In this context, it is interesting to note a difference in biblical translations. In a Protestant Swiss Bible (*Die Heilige Schrift*), Tamar is called *die geweihte Buhle*. *Buhle* means "a lover, a mistress;" it is a German word (no longer in use), which in later times took on the meaning of "a prostitute." The word *geweihte* translates as "consecrated." Therefore the description applied to Tamar, *die geweihte Buhle,* turns the sexual act into something sacred.

> And he returned to Judah, and said, I cannot find her; and also the men of the place said, that there was no harlot in this place.
>
> And Judah said, Let her take it to her, lest we be shamed: behold, I sent this kid, and thou hast not found her. (Genesis 38:22–23)

Why should he be shamed? Because he relinquished his male power, his seed, in the pledges he made to a presumed harlot.

And it came to pass about three months after, that it was told Judah, saying, Tamar thy daughter-in-law hath played the harlot; and also, behold, she is with child by whoredom. And Judah said, Bring her forth, and let her be burnt. (Genesis 38:24)

The Bible tells us that widows playing the harlot were burned. Such horrific treatment must have sprung from a fear of free, independent women in whom the divine feminine power was alive. In those times, any Israelite who "spent his seed" by having intercourse with a temple priestess in a Canaanite temple was put to death. This fact could also explain Judah's so-called shame.

When you encounter Tamar in your life journey, she captures your full attention, she turns your world upside down, she destroys your moral convictions and your belief patterns, and she makes you laugh and cry. She brings instability into your life, she challenges your established way of behaving, she brings joy and sadness, and she makes you feel beautiful, desired, and loved. She awakens your sensuality, and you become aware of your powers of seduction. Tamar makes you pregnant. But from the beginning, she also demands sacrifice, pledges, and strong commitment. There is no escape.

When she was brought forth, she sent to her father-in-law, saying, By the man, whose these are, am I with child: and she said, Discern, I pray thee, whose are these, the signet, and bracelets, and staff.

And Judah acknowledged them, and said, She hath been more righteous than I; because that I gave her not to Shelah, my son. And he knew her again no more. (Genesis 38:25–26)

"Being with child" means, in this context, to once again enter into relationship with the motherly womb, but in a new, more conscious way. Being able to discern between feminine and masculine prevents blind identification with either. Judah's admission that Tamar is more righteous than he himself indicates an acknowledgment and redemption occurring in both figures. A mutual exchange of masculine and feminine power transpires between the biblical figures, which elevates them to the two divine sources of our lives: Father and Mother.

Although Shelah, the third son of Judah, remains a shadowy figure in the background of the story, he is nonetheless an important element. He represents lack of trust. Judah was afraid of Tamar, knowing as he did of her sexual power. Shelah specifically represents a lack of trust in independent, feminine creativity, a very serious obstacle in the creative process that should not be underestimated.

> And it came to pass in the time of her travail, that, behold, twins were in her womb.
>
> And it came to pass, when she travailed, that the one put out his hand: and the midwife took and bound upon his hand a scarlet thread, saying, This came out first.
>
> And it came to pass, as he drew back his hand, that behold, his brother came out: and she said, How hast thou broken forth? This breech be upon thee: therefore his name was called Pharez.
>
> And afterward came out his brother, that had the scarlet thread upon his hand: and his name was called Zerah. (Genesis 38:27–30)

The mythologies of all cultures reflect a strong interest in the birth of twins. Quite frequently they represent two extremes, with one twin being dark and the other light, or one being good and the other evil. In Greek, *Pharez* means "to make a breach," and *Zara* in Greek and *Zerach* in Hebrew mean "splendor, brightness." These two names are mentioned in the genealogy of Jesus (Matthew 1:3) and represent the only twins in the list. It should also be mentioned, in this regard, that the number two represents polarity in relationships.

> Polarity is the loom on which reality is strung, the magnetic dance of universal forces. Within the mirror of polarity, you will find the many faces of illusion as well as the ultimate freedom from illusion.

Polarity reveals your conflicts, struggles, and the apparent separation created by your beliefs in duality. . . . Polarized positions
actually work in cooperative alliance. In cooperation, all polarities
serve as backgrounds for full appreciation of one another and the
whole.[10]

In the Bible, the twins are referred to as brothers, but I strongly sus-
pect that Zerah is a female. (In Genesis 46:17 a Zerah [Serah] is mentioned as a daughter of Asher.) She is the one with the scarlet thread on
her hand, indicating the feminine blood bond with the Goddess. During
their birth, she is the breech baby. Whether in a man or a woman, the
process of coming to soul consciousness is always initiated by the divine
feminine. The twins are the fruit of Tamar, the Palm Tree of Life, in
whom we find the polarity of masculine and feminine, emerging in the
brightness of the rising sun. The motif of the twins, when it crosses the
threshold of consciousness, manifests this double aspect.

The archetype of the twins finds beautiful expression in the oral
traditions of Mayan shamanism:

Inside the Earth Fruit level of creation, there are two simultaneous
faces of reality called the Twins: the world where we dream, and the
world where we work. To a shaman, a dream is not a creation of the
mind, psyche, or soul. It is the remembered fragment of the experience of one's natural spirit in the twin world, the dreamworld. The
twin world of dreams, like this world, never ceases living, forming
as it does a parallel continuum to the waking world. . . .

Although the landscapes of dreams may seem different from the
landscape of the awake world, it is actually the balanced opposite,
reversed version, where our souls live out our bodies' lives reenacted
as if in a complex kind of mirror. Like the two opposing wings of
a butterfly, the dreamworld is one wing and the awake world is the
other wing. The butterfly must have both wings connected at the
Heart in order to fly and function.

Neither wing—dreams or waking—contains all of life. Real life occurs as a result of the interaction of the two. The life is the butterfly's heart, and both dreaming and awake working life are necessary to keep the heart alive. Our lives, like the butterfly's heart, are kept aloft by two opposing, mirroring, twin-like wings. This heart is the third thing, the Rubux heart that all ritual seeks to feed and keep alive.[11]

The third thing is what we call "love," and that is the potent energy that unites as well as divides all relationship. It may well be that the Catholic Church continues to vehemently refuse to consecrate women as priestesses because it would be tantamount to reestablishing a relationship to the Goddess in Christianity. A similar denial can be seen in a recent instance involving the Protestant church. A female minister, the mother of five children, was denied an appointment to a parish, apparently because she was too attractive and had too much sex appeal. In spite of her acknowledged professional qualifications, she did not fit into the conservative image of how a female minister should appear. She decided not to bow to the decision of the church and instead went public with her case, which attracted international attention. Her personality united sexuality and spirituality, thus touching on the archetype of the sacred prostitute or priestess. In interviews, she mentioned that people often see her as the prostitute, the mother, the wife, and the lover: all roles that form background to her profession.

If we compare the role of the sacred prostitute of the past with the prostitute of today, the decline in the value we place on her mirrors the deterioration of our relationship with matter: how we abuse nature, how we infect her with deadly poison, and how we desecrate her continually in the name of economic interests. When we eat junk food and food that has been chemically and genetically manipulated, we are not honoring the sacred within ourselves. This same lack of honor and respect can be seen in our treatment of the maize plant, which the Mayans revere as *the* divine seed. Maize, the golden corn of the

Native American, has been denigrated from its role as a sacred object of utmost importance to the Mayans and other indigenous cultures—a relationship imbued with old traditions and highest knowledge—into the primary genetically manipulated foodstuff on our planet.[12] Our Western minds no longer grasp the fact that the earth is sacred because it is the body of the Goddess made manifest. Instead, just as the seed was wasted by the sons of Judah for personal ego-purposes, the divine seed is being used for purposes of economic greed and power.

What we are witnessing in our day is a corruption of sexuality. In her book *Sophia, Goddess of Wisdom,* Caitlín Matthews writes in the subchapter entitled "Resacrilizing the Body":

> Sexual love lies like an unexploded bomb in our society. It is poten-
> tially the most creative of acts but, robbed of its sacred dimension,
> it may also be the focus of the most destructive acts.[13]

We should also be alarmed when we consider the fact that science is developing increasingly varied, seemingly inexhaustible technical means to overcome sterility. In the face of such processes as conceptions involving five people, children à la carte, or uteri to rent, we are forced to ask what has happened to the ethics of setting limits.

The Catholic Church has always insisted on sexuality exclusively for the purpose of procreation, so for modern women, sexuality without procreation was a liberation. Today, however, we have procreation without sexuality and it is called "immaculate fecundation." Where is our Tree of Life if the fathers and mothers are unknown? Where do we find the goddess of love and sexuality in this process? This attempt on the part of science to "beat" nature also expresses the hidden unconscious belief that sexuality is sinful.

This estranged state naturally results in a state of mourning that echoes Tamar's widowhood. It may well be that the mysterious attraction of Black Madonnas seen today arises from the fact that they emanate both the unity of primal matter with spirituality *and* the hidden mourning of our soul. Poignantly, the simple soulful form of the Black Madonna at Einsiedeln in Switzerland is decked out with rich jewelry and attired in sumptuous gowns that are changed on a weekly basis. She is literally buried, imprisoned in clothing not her own. She also stands locked behind black bars, a potent and precise image of how we have imprisoned our feminine soul.

Tamar's whole story teaches us to free ourselves from the illusory conviction that we have lost touch with the archetype of the divine as a whole within ourselves. Our own personal Tree of Life needs to blossom and be fruitful on a soul level, and *that* is the fundamental goal of the sacred prostitute. As the goddess of sexual love and fertility, she is *also* the goddess of the fertility of the soul, experienced through the physical body. Tamar, the sacred prostitute, the goddess of love, reminds us that she is our heart and the one who, in her love, embraces our opposites.

SIX

Rahab
The Meretrix

The story of Rahab, told in Joshua 2:1–21 and Joshua 6, arises out of a collective soul situation as a response to the newly formed patriarchy. She appears during the time when the Hebrews were under the leadership of Joshua: successor to Moses, hero, warrior, and conqueror of the Promised Land of Canaan. The biblical story of the destruction of Jericho reminds us in an anthropomorphized form of the defeat of the cult of the Goddess in Canaan by the Hebrew invaders. Defeated the Goddess may have been, from the patriarchal standpoint, but eliminated she was not. Her image was hidden and veiled, but continued to evolve.

Despite both the apparent loss of any living link to the Great Goddess and the changes wrought by the numerous translations these mythic stories have undergone, we find the Goddess revealing herself once more as an indestructible life force in Rahab. Rahab's home is Jericho, a town situated further below sea level than any other in the world. Jericho means "town of palm trees," reminding us of "Tamar" whose name—"palm tree/Tree of Life"—clearly identifies her as a symbol of the Goddess. If we take Jericho as a symbol, we would have to say that it reflects one of the deepest layers of the psyche in which our spiritual memory of the Goddess is stored.

And Joshua the son of Nun sent out of Shittim two men to spy secretly, saying, Go view the land, even Jericho. And they went, and came into an harlot's house, named Rahab, and lodged there. (Joshua 2:1)

In an Italian version of the Bible (*La Sacra Bibbia*), Rahab is called *meretrice,* meaning "whore," but associated with "innkeeper," as these two were often housed together. Jung speaks of the *meretrix,* the whore, as a synonym in alchemy "for the *prima materia,* the *corpus imperfectum,* which is sunk into darkness," like the human being "who wanders in darkness, unconscious and unredeemed."[1]

I view this from a somewhat different perspective. The meretrix, the whore, has sunk into darkness in the sense that she has fallen into oblivion. Our *generatrix mater,* primal matter, has become an object of negative projection, of imperfection viewed as something inferior. We have lost our sense of being part of the Goddess; we have forgotten that we are created of the same substance. Dark, primal matter can thus be viewed as a state existing prior to the "fall" into duality. Seen this way, primal matter is not a state of imperfection, but on the contrary contains the whole, by embracing the polarities. This wholeness evades our comprehension, for it is veiled. This aspect of the Goddess manifests in the veiled sacred prostitute, as we have seen in Tamar's story.

Sophia, speaking as Wisdom, as Inanna once spoke in Sumeria and Isis in Egypt, says:

> For I am the first and the last,
> I am the honored one and the scorned one,
> I am the whore and the holy one . . .[2]

These are ancient words, reflecting the truth of her manifestation. The whole that embraces the opposites is represented in the time of the Judges by the meretrix, Rahab, who gives herself indiscriminately to men and who shelters and hides the two spies.

Behind the name Rahab lies the hidden, primordial power of the Goddess who, according to Job, was defeated by Yahweh:

> He divideth the sea with his power, and by his understanding he smiteth the proud.
>
> By his spirit he hath garnished the heavens; his hand hath formed the crooked serpent. (Job 26:12–13)

In an Italian version of the Bible (*La Bibbia,* Giobbe 26:12–13), in place of the word "proud" we read "Rahab." She is the personification of the primordial sea. In Hebrew, her name signifies "wild," or "stormy." As the Babylonian Tiamat, she is called "chaos," "great serpent," and "dragon," and she is goddess of the sea.

Robert Graves, in *The White Goddess,* mentions the marriage between Joshua and the goddess of the sea, who appears in the Bible as the whore Rahab. From this union, according to the *Sifre,* the oldest Midrash (rabbinic Judaic interpretation of religious texts) sprang only daughters, from whom many prophets descended, including Jeremiah. Hannah, the mother of Samuel, is also identified by the *Sifre,* as the incarnation of Rahab.

Rahab represents a powerful image of the collective unconscious: our lost relation to our collective and cosmic soul. She is the Great Whore, a title that conveys her cosmic dimension. The following remarks on religious trends during the time period in which her story transpires helps us to better understand its significance:

> The *Enuma Elish*—the Babylonian epic of creation—tells the story of the conquest and murder of the original mother goddess, Tiamat, by the god Marduk, her great-great-great-grandson . . .
>
> The Iron Age (beginning ca. 1250 BC) saw the completion of the process begun in the Bronze Age in which numinosity was transferred from the Mother Goddess to the Father God. The *Enuma Elish* is the first story of a replacing of a mother goddess who gen-

erates creation as part of herself by a god who "makes" creation as something separate from himself.[3]

The same theme appears in Genesis, as we well know, where we find a male god as the lone creator. Such phrases as "the earth was without form, and void; and darkness was upon the face of the deep . . . and the spirit of God moved upon the face of the waters" (Genesis 1:2) remind us of the sea goddess, Rahab-Tiamat, who stands at the beginning of creation. In Genesis darkness is attributed to "the deep."

> Blackness is an image long associated with the Great Goddesses: Isis, Cybele, Demeter and Artemis. It symbolizes the ineffable wisdom and mystery of life and its power to regenerate itself. . . . But during the Iron Age, as the goddess was replaced by the god, blackness came to be a symbol of darkness in the sense of evil.[4]

The darkness of the deep could suggest a kinship with the concept in physics of black or heavy matter, and with chaos theory. The theologian Matthew Fox and biologist Rupert Sheldrake, in their book, *The Physics of Angels, Exploring the Realm Where Science and Religion Meet,* say that physics seems to have discovered the cosmic unconscious, which is called "dark matter" and is completely unknown to us. It seems that dark matter is "supernatural" because it is not subject to the natural laws discovered by humans. Fox and Sheldrake's statement that chaos differs from order only by the fact that it contains a more subtle pattern bears a striking resemblance to our primordial creatrix, called "chaos" or "dragon," with her invisible ordering principle in our psyche. In light of Rahab's symbolism, the terms "dark matter" and "cosmic unconscious" are interchangeable with "Mother Goddess"—that is, with "primordial creatrix/*meretrix*"—if only we can reverse our predominately rational state of mind.

Here it is important to read the hidden messages of the Goddess revealed to us through the symbols of the palm tree and the town of palm trees. She is telling us she has not vanished from our souls, because our souls are her dwelling place. We need to redeem her memory, a memory that is imprinted in our genealogical Tree of Life or, in modern terms, in our spiritual DNA, in which the four building blocks—similar to the fourfold structure of the psyche, embodied by our four women—form the elements of the genetic code of the soul through which hereditary information is transmitted and transcribed.

The myth also indicates another level of meaning more directly related to the psyche of that time. Symbolically, the struggle between the hero (Joshua) and the serpent dragon (Rahab the meretrix from the town of Jericho) represents the power of human consciousness as it struggles to gain mastery over instinctual and unconscious patterns of behavior.

> Where the hero myth is perceived in terms of the growth of consciousness, it becomes an inner quest for illumination. Here the conflict is not so much between good and evil, but rather one between a greater or a lesser understanding. The "dragon" is then ignorance or unconsciousness, not so much chaos as the fear of it.[5]

From this standpoint, the words of Job quoted above take on another meaning: ". . . he divided the sea [that is, ignorance, unconsciousness] with his power [consciousness] and by his understanding he smiteth through the proud [Rahab, the dragon]." The hero Joshua thus embodies the experience of the masculine quest of the hero, an archetypal journey for both women *and* men to undertake:

> The symbolic significance of the hero myth for us . . . is that the hero is the embodiment of the archetypal masculine in *all* human beings—the questing consciousness in search of a goal.[6]

But what is the symbolic significance of the heroine's quest represented by Rahab the meretrix? Paralleling the hero's quest is a feminine quest—a quest that has never been honored or acknowledged—that of redeeming the memory of our cosmic mother. This is an archetypal journey awaiting women and men alike. As we have seen, feminine consciousness has been riven from masculine consciousness from the beginnings of the Iron Age down to the present. The Father God displaced the Mother Goddess and, in splitting spirit off from nature, corrupted her, changing her from a life-giving mother to a death-dealing dragon. The goal of the heroine's quest is to restore the lost wholeness in which Mother Goddess and Father God are brought together in a more harmonic relation to one another, in a new myth.

We could then say that the hero or heroine is the embodiment of the archetypal masculine-feminine in all human beings; the questing *totality of consciousness* in search of a new goal. In this sense, we need to integrate the heroine's quest. This is what is embodied by Rahab, the archetypal feminine as soul-teacher. "One of the ways in which consciousness evolves is through the differentiation of what was once experienced as a unity."[7] We could reverse this and say that one of the ways consciousness evolves now is through the reexperiencing of the lost original unity.

In this context, the symbolism of the names of the two spies who stay with Rahab is revealing. *In Sagen der Juden,* one is called Pinehas and the other Kaleb. Kaleb means "dog."

In *The Myth of the Goddess* we read:

> The dog is one of the most ancient animals belonging to the goddess as the guardian of her mysteries. In Greece dogs were sacred to Hecate, goddess of the dark phase of the moon and so of the crossroads and the underworld. The culture of Old Europe reveals the very ancient origin of the link between dog, dark moon, black night, and goddess. . . . On vases from Cucuteni (eastern Rumania and western Ukraine) dogs guard a tree, centrally placed to signify the Tree of Life.
>
> The Neolithic images are the earliest to show the relationship

between these guardian animals and the tree that once symbolized the goddess herself.[8]

The dog also represents instinctual orientation and intuition. We use the phrases "to have a good nose for something" or "to follow one's nose," attributes needed to be a good spy or explorer. Pinehas, the other explorer, tells Rahab, as she tries to hide them on the roof of her house, that he is a priest, and that a priest is similar to an angel: when he so deems, he is seen, and when he so deems, he remains invisible. The priest-angel is also a mediator, and hence found at the opposite, more spiritual end of the psychic spectrum from the more instinctual "dog."

Together, Pinehas and Kaleb represent both ends of the spectrum in which matter (physiology) lies at one pole and spirit at the other; they remind us not to eliminate instinctual nature from the spiritual in the process of becoming conscious. Jung once compared the human psyche to the color band, which at the red pole loses itself in instinct and somatic processes, whereas at the ultraviolet pole it extends into the sphere of the archetypes, which is the realm of the spirit. The archetypal images manifest the sense of instinct, its hidden intention, as Jung points out.

What kind of hidden intention, then, do the archetypal images of the dog and priest-angel indicate? The dog belongs to the Goddess as the guardian of her mysteries. That means that to gain access to her original, transformative, creative power, we need divine instinctive intuition. The priest-angel belongs to the realm of the spirit and symbolizes vision, illumination, and inspiration independent of the will. They appear in their own time, choosing themselves whether to remain latent or become manifest. This is the well-known and fully recognized reality of the creative process. They represent eyes that can see in the dark, which intuit the symbolic pathway to resurrect (or restore) the memory of the Goddess. To restore the spiritual memory of the Goddess we need divine instinctive intuition: vision, illumination, and inspiration.

In Joshua 2:6, we are told that Rahab hides the spies with stalks of flax, which she has laid out on the roof. Stalks of flax were typically laid out in the sun after being macerated in water. The spinning of flax is connected with feminine activities. Sowing, spinning, and weaving represent feminine life and creativity. Through Rahab the meretrix, the great creatrix emerges, she who is eternally sowing, spinning, and weaving life eternal out of her own being. These feminine activities can represent the invisible ordering principle in the psyche called "chaos." However,

> [i]n our culture there still exists a prejudice against the deeper instinctive layers of the psyche on the grounds that they are non-rational, chaotic and uncontrollable—qualities that have been designated as "feminine"—together with the assumption that the only ordering principle in the psyche comes from the "masculine" exercise of "reason," which can formulate the laws of consciousness capable of intellectual definition. . . .[9]

In the legend, Pinehas and Kaleb disguise themselves as peddlers of pots. It is interesting to note that one of the Sumero-Babylonian titles for the Great Goddess was "the Potter," also called Aruru the Great, who first created human beings out of clay. The fact that the two explorers in the legend are disguised as peddlers of pots could thus be read as meaning that they "disguised" their close connection to the Goddess.

There is an interesting annotation by von Ranke Graves and Patai in reference to the myth of Judah and Tamar. According to these authors, Hosea 11:12 can be read as indicating that Judah turned away from God, while remaining faithful to the q'deshim ("holy ones"). This can be understood to mean that he broke away from his brothers and adopted the religious customs of the Canaanites, in which the cult of the q'deshim was included. The q'deshim were kelebites or "dog-priests," that is, male prostitutes in the guise of women. The admission of Caleb into the tribe of Judah supports this interpretation, as does

Judah's uninhibited intercourse with a *kedesha,* or sacred prostitute. The dog-priest bears witness to the continuity of sacred prostitution in the cult of the Goddess. The feminine attire donned by priests and monks can be seen as a final echo of the original androgynous nature of the Goddess. Since the dog-priests were sent by Joshua, we could surmise that Joshua also had a connection to the Goddess, which included his quest for the feminine principle.

We stand on the threshold of a new understanding of Rahab's mysteries, but we cannot redeem her memory without first confronting what has been termed "the dragon." This dragon is a composite of our illusion of successful suppression of the feminine instinctual nature, dogmatic religious convictions, projections, repressed emotions and thoughts, fears, anger, lack of faith in our own creativity, and loss of trust and faith. This "dragon" represents a negative psychic substrata, accumulated layer by layer over thousands of years, which has caused—and still causes—considerable suffering for women and men and is confronting us today in the destruction of nature, climatic changes, prostitution in its myriad forms, gene manipulation, and new strains of illnesses. These problems with the environment and in society are a consequence of the lost unity of nature and spirit. Baring and Cashford underscore the importance of the seminal change in imagery that occurred in Babylonia in the Iron Age.

> [This change in imagery] has influenced the Judaeo-Christian view of nature, matter and whatever else has been defined as feminine, and it has structured our paradigm images in mythology, religion, literature, science, and psychology. Here, in its earliest formulation, the idea is precisely articulated and embodied in myth: that what is feminine is chaotic, destructive, demonic, and is to be feared and mastered.[10]

In order to change the formulation, to articulate and realize a new myth (or to rearticulate the oldest one!), what is feminine has to be recognized as the physical fundament of life, which represents our deepest, most vital bond to the Great Mother. This is an experience that can only be had through the physical body, which the sacred prostitute teaches us.

Once, while trying to penetrate a labyrinth (the symbol of our journey through life), walking stick in hand, I was taken by the urge to hack my way through it, just as if I were in a jungle. I realized that I was, in fact, vigorously cutting through all my doubts, insecurities, and fears. As I did so I felt that my actions were guided by a loving force so powerful that it moved me to tears. Upon reaching the center of the labyrinth, I offered up my stick to the force, in a gesture of complete surrender. As I traversed the spiral outward, I grasped the stick with a new sense of power, one having nothing to do with the ego, but rather with the sensation that the stick had been transformed into a cross. It was a sign that the battle of life is won in the name of infinite whole love. The power of complete love without beginning or end is the hidden treasure of the dragon.

This was not an abstract experience, but rather one that involved my whole body: my feet were acutely aware of the soft ground beneath them, and I felt the decisive strength in the muscles of my arm as it gripped the stick, the bitter tears coursing down my cheeks, the sharp physical pain in my heart as it was torn apart by separation, and an exploding joy irradiating my entire body as I danced out the connection with the eternal rhythm of love.

The hero's quest remains incomplete when the heroine, the archetypal feminine in both genders, is left behind. This is clearly reflected, for example, in the myth of Ariadne and Theseus, when he abandons her on the island of Naxos. Women are greatly endangered when they delegate or give away their power to the masculine. Ariadne's red thread is a symbol of her blood bond to the Goddess, and this is the power and bond she relinquishes to Theseus. Theseus' journey becomes a purely masculine quest, while Ariadne loses her power and the feminine outlook sinks into the unconscious. No true transformation and evolution of consciousness takes place, a fact that continues to detrimentally influence our current culture.

Theseus needs Ariadne because she is the link, the thread to the deepest layers of the soul with all their hidden treasures. Kerényi calls Ariadne "the archetypal reality of soulgiving." Ariadne needs Theseus not because of his ability to kill, but because of his capacity to channel and redirect redeemed and liberated psychic power (libido). There are moments in the life of the psyche when we stand poised on the verge of a new consciousness, facing the "dragon" or the "Minotaur," creatures from another world, guardians of the threshold, the center where the hidden treasure lies. In such crucial situations, it is the feminine principle that knows the way and is the torchbearer; it is her eyes that can pierce the darkness. We need to rewrite the story so that Ariadne walks hand in hand with Theseus and they face the task together, united by the power of their love.

While there is no analogous quest in the myth of Rahab, there is a link between her legend and that of Ariadne: the red thread or cord, which appears in Rahab's story as the life force. When a search is under way for the two spies she is hiding, Rahab says to them:

> I know that the Lord hath given you the land, and that your terror is fallen upon us, and that all the inhabitants of the land faint because of you. . . . [F]or the Lord your God, he is God in heaven above, and in earth beneath. (Joshua 2:9, 11)

Rahab is speaking of the shift of consciousness in which the Mother Goddess of the great above and the great below was replaced by the Father God, who became lord of heaven and earth and inflicted terror upon the people of that period. As Baring and Cashford write, the Book of Joshua

> reflects the values of the Hebrews who recorded it. The deficient morality of Yahweh becomes more understandable when his com-

mands are taken not as divine revelations, but as "revelations" of Iron-Age values and patriarchal customs reflected in the behavior of kings, priests, and prophets.[11]

In any interpretation of this material, it is vital to listen to the voice of the soul as represented by Rahab.

Now therefore, I pray you, swear unto me by the Lord, since I have shewed you kindness, that ye will also shew kindness unto my father's house, and give me a true token:

And that ye will save alive my father and my mother, and my brethren, and my sisters, and all that they have, and deliver our lives from death.

And the men answered her, Our life for yours, if ye utter not this our business. And it shall be, when the Lord hath given us the land that we will deal kindly and truly with thee.

Then she let them down by a cord through the window. . . .

And the men said unto her, We will be blameless of this thine oath which thou hast made us swear.

Behold, when we come into the land, thou shalt bind this line of scarlet thread in the window which thou didst let us down by. . . . (Joshua 2:12–18)

Unlike Ariadne, Rahab does not give away her power; rather, she defines herself and her "tree-of-life family" through the scarlet thread. This bond for life transpires between Rahab, the meretrix, and a dog-priest identified as a male prostitute, who symbolizes feminine and masculine soul images. We experience these as polarities, yet they remind us of the original androgynous unity of the Goddess.

The archetypal feminine is rendered in mythology as a figure of the goddess who was originally androgynous, that is, she was both female and male in the metaphorical sense that she was both the womb and the generative force that seeded new forms of life within it, which she brought forth as the universe.[12]

Rahab and the dog-priest represent our soul twins; the same twins mentioned at the end of Tamar's story. A soul twin is the closest "other-you," embodying the deepest yearning of the soul. It is the blood kinship of the heart.

Before conquering the town of Jericho, Joshua had a significant experience. He encountered a man with a drawn sword. Joshua approached him and asked:

> Art thou for us, or for our adversaries?
>   And he said, Nay; but as captain of the host of the Lord I am now come. And Joshua fell on his face to the earth, and did worship and said unto him, What saith my lord unto his servant?
>   And the captain of the Lord's host said unto Joshua, Loose thy shoe from off thy foot; for the place whereon you standest is holy. And Joshua did so. (Joshua 5:13–15)

This captain of the host of the Lord is an angel who had been promised from God to his chosen people as guide and leader in the conquest of the Promised Land (Exodus 23:20).

Joshua seems to be expressing here his complete surrender to and respect for the holy ground. He is entering the realm of the "town of the palm tree," that is, of the Great Mother. We could call it the "territory of the dragon," as a metaphor for the price demanded by the unconscious for conquering it. Removing one's shoes could be interpreted as the sacrifice of the personal egotistical standpoint to a higher holy power. Joshua is the hero in search of a new understanding. His actions suggest a desire for a strong relationship to the feminine principle. In *Die Sagen der Juden* we read that Rahab married Joshua, which further supports the idea that the union of the feminine and the masculine in our psyche leads to a new form of consciousness.

Two movements can be discerned in the Lord's commands to Joshua prior to the battle of Jericho: one circular and the other, after the collapse of the walls, a straight line:

> And the Lord said unto Joshua, See, I have given into thine hand Jericho. . . .
>
> And ye shall compass the city, all ye men of war, and go round about the city once. Thus shalt thou do six days.
>
> And seven priests shall bear before the ark seven trumpets of rams' horns: and the seventh day ye shall compass the city seven times, and the priests shall blow with the trumpets.
>
> And it shall come to pass, that when they make a long blast with the ram's horn, and when ye hear the sound of the trumpet, all the people shall shout with a great shout; and the wall of the city shall fall down flat, and the people shall ascend up every man straight before him. (Joshua 6:2–5)

The orders given to Joshua to encircle Jericho express the mysterious circular movement set in motion in our soul when we search for new awareness. We are extracting a "piece of land" from the unconscious. Jung states:

> The circulation is not merely movement in a circle, but means, on the one hand, the marking off of the sacred precinct and, on the other, fixation and concentration. . . . The circular movement thus has the moral significance of activating the light and dark forces of human nature, and together with them all psychological opposites of whatever kind they may be. It is nothing less than self-knowledge by means of self-brooding. . . .[13]

Jung regards the circle as a symbol of the soul and the Self. It is one of the primary feminine symbols, as opposed to the line and the cross, which represent the masculine spirit. Erich Neumann, in examining the symbolic significance of differences between matriarchal and patriarchal consciousness, observes that the circular and brooding spiritual activity of matriarchal consciousness has none of the directedness of the act of thinking, neither of deduction nor of critical judgment. Matriarchal consciousness is more interested in the meaningfulness of things than in facts and data. Its wisdom is paradoxical: rather than clearly dividing the opposites, splitting them off from, and opposing them to one another, as patriarchal consciousness does, it binds them together in an "as well as."

The divine instructions given to Joshua mirror a spiritual activity in which feminine and masculine consciousnesses are united. The result is that the feminine soul-giving aspect represented by Rahab awakens the soul to spiritual life through the power of infinite love (the red thread).

Other symbols appearing in the story support this interpretation. The number seven is a sacred number held to possess mystical power, being a number of completion, representing the union of the female (four) with the male (three). The ark is a symbol of the maternal womb, a place of union and transformation. The blare of the trumpet is a signal to people to assemble and draw on their spiritual power together. The horn of the ram has a dual significance: in its shape and assertiveness it embodies the dynamic male principle, whereas its hollowness can simultaneously represent the receptive feminine. It therefore also stands for a well-balanced and mature attitude in the psyche.

In summary, these symbols affirm that we need a balanced psychic attitude when undergoing a process of transformation, when we undertake a quest. We have to unite our feminine and masculine consciousness, to concentrate all our energies on mobilizing our spiritual forces. Then the walls erected by our illusions, fears, projections, and all that we have repressed crumble, the fake dragon dwindles away, and we are ready for the transition from one understanding to another; we are prepared to meet the unknown, the true dragon.

The key symbol in this process is the ark. The maternal womb is our profound, committed religious attitude, our willingness to let go of ego desires, our complete trust and abandonment to a higher design. It is the recognition, in trembling, of the power of love: all this is the virgin matrix/meretrix in which the divine seed can ripen and come to fruition.

To enter the town of Jericho is to step into the realm of the transpersonal soul. It is the experience of beginning to grasp that we are an intrinsic part of a greater whole and at the same time, paradoxically, the revelation of our true identity.

But the story presents what transpired in a very different light:

> And they utterly destroyed all that was in the city, both man and woman, young and old, and ox, and sheep, and ass, with the edge of the sword. (Joshua 6:21)

If we view this as a patriarchal consciousness, it reflects the deficient morality of the Hebrews of that period. They disregarded the angel's command to honor the hallowed ground. But the question arises: "Are we any better today?" This is the danger when entering the archetypal dimension with the rational mind, the "impatient sword of comprehension," which can smite down all the new possibilities we encounter on our quest. The sword signifies forcefulness and power. It can also be the vital new impetus to clear a path so that we can recognize a greater reality. When we reach a threshold, the double-edged sword presents us with the choice of either defeating or acknowledging and redeeming the power embodied in Rahab, the "dragon."

The power of love is the treasure hidden by the dragon. The sword can channel love, guiding the energy of the dragon rather than killing it. Joshua recognized this when he saved Rahab.

> But Joshua said unto the two men that had spied out the country,
> Go into the harlot's house, and bring out thence the woman, and all
> that she hath, as ye sware unto her.

> And Joshua *saved* [my italics] Rahab the harlot alive, and her
> father's household, and all that she had; and she dwelleth in Israel
> even unto this day; because she hid the messengers, which Joshua
> sent to spy out Jericho. (Joshua 6:22, 25)

In light of the above quotation, it is interesting to note the etymol-
ogy of Joshua's name: in Latin Josua, in Hebrew Jeshoshua or Jeschua,
in Greek Jesu or Jason, which all translate as "generous" or "saved."
What could this mean on a symbolic level? The dog-priest (or sacred
male prostitute), the masculine and feminine soul images, twins, intu-
itions, visions, and instinct are all qualities of the soul: they represent
polarities *and*, at the same time, the union of these very opposites.

The key to achieving this balance lies hidden in the symbolism of
the accursed spoils of war taken by Achan of the tribe of Joshua. Before
they had entered the city, Joshua had warned his people:

> And the city shall be accursed, even it, and all that are therein, to
> the Lord: only Rahab the harlot shall live, she and all that are with
> her in the house, because she hid the messengers that we sent.
>
> And ye, in any wise, keep yourselves from the accursed thing, lest
> ye make yourselves accursed, when ye take of the accursed thing,
> and make the camp of Israel a curse, and trouble it.
>
> But all the silver and gold, and vessels of brass and iron, are con-
> secrated unto the Lord: they shall come into the treasury of the
> Lord. (Joshua 6:17–19)

After Jericho was burnt to the ground, only the silver, gold, and
vessels of brass and iron were placed in the treasure house of the Lord.

> But the children of Israel committed a trespass in the accursed
> thing: for Achan . . . took the accursed thing: and the anger of the
> Lord was kindled against the children of Israel. (Joshua 7:1)

The meaning of the word "accursed" is also "execrable," which means "to take away the sacred character." The Greek interdiction is "anathema," meaning "gift of consecration," but it was later changed by St. Paul to mean "accursed," and anathema has become the official ecclesiastic term for excommunication. In following the transformation in meaning of just this one word, we can illustrate what happened in the Iron Age as the sacred character of the Great Goddess slipped away.

The thief Achan was first stoned to death then burned with his entire family. The stolen, "accursed," objects, according to the Bible, were a Babylonian coat, two hundred shekels of silver, and a wedge of gold worth fifty gold shekels. According to the Hebrew legend, Achan also took an object called a Teraphim. The Teraphim must have been a cult object, but its function is not clear in the Old Testament. According to Patai, however, "there is ample archaeological evidence as to the importance of Asherah as a household goddess, a variety of the Teraphim."[14] It represents small divine figures or possibly a cult mask used as a harbinger of oracles. If we regard the Teraphim as an oracular device, it could well represent an object used in the mysteries of the Goddess to initiate a religious act. The Latin word *oraculu(m)* derives from *orare,* which means "to pray."

The suggestion that the Teraphim might also represent a divine figure or mask is quite interesting. In his essay "Mankind and Mask," Karl Kerényi states that "the main function of the mask is unifying transformation or, still better, transformative union."[15] The mask hides and it frightens, but above all it creates a relationship between the person and the being it represents.[16] It is an encounter between a human being and the face of the impersonal—be it divine or bestial, heroic or mundane. It is a way of encountering the archetype.

The human countenance, which usually bears the stamp of individual features, the features of a "personality" (from the Latin word for "mask," *persona*) becomes here the expression of the general and the collective. The position of the human being—between individual existence and a broader, Proteus-like self, able to take on all and any forms—is made visible through the mask. It is a true apparatus of magic that enables a person to become aware of his or her situation at all times, and to find the way into a great spiritual world without leaving the natural world.[17] But this momentous identification has to be dispelled, otherwise an inflated sense of power would grip the psyche. This is the danger that ensues when we encounter the dragon.

Silver as a white metal is a symbol of purity. From ancient Sumeria to medieval alchemy, it has been associated with the moon and femininity. In the language of Christian symbolism, it represents the purified soul. In the Psalms, the words of God are compared with silver. The Babylonian coat is a yet another link to the myth of Tiamat. It is a symbol of protection and of prophetic power. It is also an attribute of the Madonna and of Rahab, according to the Hebrew legend.

The "gold shekels" become a "golden tongue" in the Hebrew legend. The golden tongue is often associated with the flame because of its form and agility. It is the organ that shapes words into a constructively powerful force, or into a destructive one. Gold is an incorruptible metal and a solar symbol associated with the masculine principle.

Achan's act of stealing the consecrated, cursed objects was heroic, for they were a symbolic "message-in-a-bottle" from the Great Goddess. Achan brought these symbols, which represent a mystical process, out of the unconscious and into consciousness. Thus the Teraphim symbolizes the beginning of a religious act in which the face of the mask conceals the mystery of the event, but at the same time reveals its transpersonal aspect. The Babylonian coat represents a protective religious attitude, possibly in the form of a feminine prophetic mediating power. This is the power of Rahab.

The place of the transformative union is the purified human soul, symbolized by the silver. Gold is the immortal transcendent element because it is incorruptible. We might say that the golden tongue is the eternal, incorruptible, divine language of the soul, a language that is able to unite values of both genders in revealing its wisdom. That language is only revealed in the world of symbols, like those that abound in the story of Rahab, which teaches us to achieve a consciousness more ample and profound. We need to consider both ways of female and male consciousness, because we can conquer new land only when they are united. This is the essence of Rahab's message. She is a culture bringer.

SEVEN

Ruth

Redeeming the Soul

I read the Book of Ruth at the age of sixteen, when my godmother gave me a Bible as a confirmation present. I remember not liking Ruth's pledge to Naomi, finding it too dramatically sentimental and too threatening to my sense of freedom. It is quite significant that much later my godmother's gift urged me to search for the lost "God-Mother" in the Old Testament *and* that the sense of a threat to my freedom engendered a deep life commitment, which is what Ruth's pledge really is. I once read that a first name holds power and it is not given to you by chance. As a young girl I was not fond of my name, which means "companion," but later I felt a strong bond with my namesake. I often feel her at my side as an invisible friend, especially in those moments when I find it difficult to be truthful to my innermost self. The result is a feeling of returning home, to the home of the heart. And indeed, Ruth's story is about just that.

The Book of Ruth is inserted between Judges and I Samuel. It is called the jewel of the Old Testament. The book is divided in four chapters, reminding us of the fourfold structure of our soul: 1) the devoted daughter-in- law and returning home, 2) the gleaning, 3) the night on the threshing floor, and 4) the wedding of Ruth and Boaz.

1. THE DEVOTED DAUGHTER-IN-LAW AND RETURNING HOME

At the beginning of the story, we are told that the judges have decreed that there is famine in the land, and a man named Elimelech travels, with his wife Naomi and their two sons Mahlon and Chilion, from Bethlehem to the country of Moab. It is ironic to note that Bethlehem—*bet lechem*—literally means "house of bread." Bread is one of the most important foods and at the same time is a symbol of spiritual nourishment. Jesus was born in Bethlehem, and bread later took on a most holy significance in the eucharistic transformation. The story of Ruth is one of transformation, symbolizing the gate to a spiritual realm where physical motherhood is transformed into spiritual motherhood.

Ruth, like Tamar and Rahab, is a spiritual foremother of Jesus and, also like them, is not a Hebrew. She is the *Urform*, the first manifestation, of Christic soul consciousness. With Christic soul consciousness, I mean a spiritual truth that has its roots in the four women. Ruth is the first who descended her redeemed soul experience into the earth. In this sense, she could be a prefiguration of the female aspect of Christic soul consciousness that needs to be integrated. Ruth manifests this Christic soul consciousness through love.

In *Die Sagen der Juden,* we are told that Elimelech was one of the men responsible for providing nourishment for his people, but he fled when the famine struck because he did not want to share his provisions or take on responsibility. The image conveyed here is one of spiritual hunger, a loss of relationship to the Great Mother who provides nourishment through the individual soul (Tamar) and collective cosmic soul (Rahab). Metaphorically speaking, the soul has been exiled from the human heart. It has been "sundered" from the divine.

The spiritual hunger being portrayed remains today, when the objective problem of hunger and the many people exiled from their homelands due to wars, poverty, and climatic disasters mirror in an alarming way the landscape of our inner collective soul.

The biblical story tells us:

And Elimelech Naomi's husband died; and she was left, and her two sons.

And they took them wives of the women of Moab; the name of the one was Orpah, and the name of the other Ruth: and they dwelled there about ten years.

And Mahlon and Chilion died also both of them; and the woman was left of her two sons and her husband. (Ruth 1:3–5)

The name "Elimelech" means "My God is king." This suggests that the dominant male image of God that ruled the collective consciousness of that time no longer nurtured the soul. The deaths speak to us of the deaths the exiled soul has to go through on its homeward path to the divine.

"Ten years they dwelled there." Ten years point to a fulfillment, a coming full circle, the completion of a cycle, and a return to the One in the sense of a renewed image of the divine in its *wholeness*.

Then she arose with her daughters-in-law, that she might return from the country of Moab: for she had heard in the country of Moab how that the Lord had visited his people in giving them bread. (Ruth 1:6)

The contact with the divine has been resurrected here. When our souls arise and turn homeward, then the One comes to meet us in a reciprocal gesture that nourishes us spiritually.

Wherefore she went forth out of the place where she was, and her two daughters-in-law with her; and they went on the way to return unto the land of Judah. (Ruth 1:7)

Naomi and her daughters-in-law are one and the same; they represent manifestations of the soul. Ruth and Orpah represent daughters by divine and not by human law. Naomi, as an image of the exiled human soul, went through death and sorrow, and acquired a new awareness of the feminine reality of the soul. The daughters are therefore soul images experienced as feminine. They incorporate qualities of the One, and in this sense they are divine. The story goes on to tell us that Naomi implored Orpah and Ruth to return home to their mothers and gods.

But why should Naomi implore them to return home? Her plea is, in truth, that they not lose the reestablished connection to the Great Mother. "To return" is an oft-used expression in the Book of Ruth, appearing eight times, which suggests infinite aspects and means of return to the one self. There is no time limit imposed on the return to the divine; we are always welcome. Another interesting phenomenon is that there are two movements: a return to the land of Judah, the land of the father, and a return to the mother. Orpah, whose name means "the one who turned her back," represents the unbroken thread to the mother's house and bespeaks that mysterious force that reconnects us consciously to our original source, thereby ensuring the continuity of feminine spiritual life. Yet in reality, no split occurs in turning-returning to the divine. That exists only in our dualistic minds. To return to the Father is at the same time to return to the Mother. "Home" means consciousness of the Wholeness.

Before Orpah turned back, she and Ruth ". . . lifted up their voice and wept again" (Ruth 1:14). Their weeping expresses humankind's need for a connection with something deeper. It is the lament of the parted. It is the *not-knowing* "I am divine!"

Naomi, addressing her daughters-in-law as "my daughters," says:

Turn again, my daughters: why will ye go with me? are there yet any more sons in my womb, that they will be your husbands? (Ruth 1:11)

Clearly, Naomi is indicating that the story is about the process of transforming physical into spiritual motherhood—something I experienced in my own life. Just at the time I was embarking on my work with this biblical material, my uterus had to be removed. I felt an unmistakable shift of energy in my body from physical to spiritual creativity.

Let us listen to Ruth's pledge to Naomi after Orpah's departure:

And Ruth said, Entreat me not to leave thee, or to return from following after thee: for wither thou goest, I will go: and where thou lodgest, I will lodge: thy people shall be my people, and thy God my God:

Where thou diest, will I die, and there will I be buried: the Lord do so to me, and more also, if ought but death part thee and me. (Ruth 1:16–17)

Ruth's plea is an act of submission to and alignment with divine will, which amounts to unconditional love. She places her life power in the service of love. Naomi-Ruth represents the energy of a love able to bring the soul back home. The sense of inseparability expressed here by Ruth reveals her profound connection with Naomi, who is called Naomi's *daughter* as the symbol of a newly, and consciously discovered feminine soul image on its way home. As a daughter she is able to bring forth new life, to ensure the continuity of the indestructible life force. She is soul mate, friend, and companion, as her name indicates.

Naomi is an image of the eternal soul mother from whom we never really become separated; we just lose the conscious connection to her. It is interesting to note that in *Die Sagen der Juden,* Ruth is not called "daughter- in-law," but *die Schnur,* which means "cord, rope."

When she saw that she was steadfastly minded to go with her, then she left speaking unto her.

So they two went until they came to Bethlehem. And it came

to pass, when they were come to Bethlehem, that all the city was moved about them, and they said, Is this Naomi?

And she said unto them, Call me not Naomi, call me Mara: for the Almighty hath dealt very bitterly with me.

I went out full, and the Lord has brought me home again empty: then why call me Naomi, seeing the Lord hath testified against me, and the Almighty hath afflicted me?

So Naomi returned, and Ruth the Moabitess her daughter-in-law, with her, which returned out of the country of Moab: and they came to Bethlehem in the beginning of barley harvest. (Ruth 1:18–22)

The time of harvest hints at experiences garnered in the course of life that mature the soul; we reap the fruits of these experiences through enduring sorrows, separations, delusions, and losses, and transforming them into wisdom.

"All the city was moved about them, and they said, Is this Naomi?" The journey homeward activates forces in the soul, which are recognized as belonging to oneself.

Naomi cries out "Call me not Naomi" (which means "fair, lovely, graceful"); "call me Mara" (which means "bitter") "for the Almighty hath dealt very bitterly with me. I went out full, and the Lord has brought me home again empty . . ."

In alchemy, bitterness is a quality of the salt that is the mysterious third substance needed to catalyze the union of the opposite properties of philosophical sulphur (the masculine principle) and philosophical mercury (the feminine principle). Salt is a symbol of the wisdom of love, of Eros, acquired through experience of strong and deep sentiments. The salt of wisdom is a mystical principle of the world.

Naomi's emptiness describes the soul's need to let go of the demands of the ego. The womb's virginity is essential for it to receive the divine seed. In the words of Rumi:

Try and be a sheet of paper with nothing on it.

> Be a spot of ground where nothing is growing,
> where something might be planted,
> a seed, possibly, from the Absolute.[1]

2. THE GLEANING

Naomi-Ruth and Boaz are protagonists in the process of the union of opposites in the alchemy of the soul, the only place where the image of the divine can become whole.

> And Naomi had a kinsman of her husband's, a mighty man of wealth, of the family of Elimelech; and his name was Boaz.
> And Ruth the Moabitess said unto Naomi, Let me now go to the field, and glean ears of corn after him in whose sight I shall find grace. And she said unto her, Go, my daughter. (Ruth 2:1–2)

Boaz is the son of Rahab, according to Matthean genealogy, and a descendent of Tamar's son, Perez. The name Boaz means "there is power in him," and the Bible says that he is a mighty man of wealth. Viewed from a symbolic perspective, this power and wealth is the legacy of his mother. He is the son of the soul image of the Great Mother, just as Ruth is the soul's daughter. Boaz and Ruth complement each other, even though we experience them as opposites in our souls.

In *Die Sagen der Juden,* we are informed that on the day Naomi returned with Ruth to Bethlehem, Boaz's wife died: "A woman left Bethlehem, and a new one arrived in Bethlehem." This hints at the death of the old feminine soul image, just as the death of Naomi's husband Elimelech suggests the death of the old masculine soul image before a new one can emerge.

The sickle wielded by Death in the well-known symbol is a harvesting tool, which signifies cutting through old entanglements, patterns, and fears. Cutting the ripe corn is a metaphor for the end of life; at the same time, corn is a symbol of basic sustenance. Here, it is the nourishment of the soul and the seed of new life. The images in Ruth's story thus show us that death means release, detachment, and the surrender of the ego so new life can emerge. What seems a contradiction is in fact an expression of the profound mystery of the infinite life cycles, in which life and death are a unity. The more we are able to die during our lives, the more we create new life. This view is only possible through the soul's reality.

Behind Naomi and Ruth we can also perceive the images of Demeter, "the Corn Mother, goddess of the golden harvests and the fertility of the ploughed earth, and Persephone, her daughter, the Corn Maiden, the seed in whom the corn, her mother, is continually reborn."[2] But the image of the Corn Maiden is, as we know from the myth, an unredeemed image, as she is imprisoned by Hades and dependent upon her mother.

When we consider our own time of great change and transition, what we mainly see is death and destruction. What is less evident is the new life emerging, a new consciousness of life and death as a unity, a consciousness that is no longer directed by the needs of the ego. It will give us access to a unified divine principle in our souls, which will manifest a wisdom far greater than our dualistic, materialistic thinking.

Ruth said to Naomi "Let me go now to the field, and glean ears of corn after him in whose sight I shall find grace" (Ruth 2:2). The word harvest refers to the cutting of corn in general, while *glean* is more specific, meaning "to pick up from the shorn field those ears that have escaped the harvest." What does this mean in Ruth's story? It is telling us "Take only what is given, not what you wish you had. Recognize what is, because that is the blessing." The ego wants more, and it is never satisfied. The gleaning of what belongs to you by divine will is an act of opening to grace. Grace is something that is bestowed upon us, and it is linked with work.

In the legend, we are told that Ruth picked up the corn if one or two ears lay together, but if there were three, she left them untouched as property not belonging to her. This attitude expresses a deep humility, which did not go unnoticed by Boaz. The number three could also be a metaphor for harmonized love: in the Tarot, the number three is the Empress, "the principle of love with wisdom . . . a symbol . . . which shows heart and mind having equal balance and proportion."[3]

> And she went, and came, and gleaned in the field after the reapers;
> and her hap was to light on a part of the field belonging unto Boaz,
> who was of the kindred of Elimelech. (Ruth 2:3)

It was not mere chance that Ruth happened to be gleaning in the field owned by Boaz. It is explained by the attraction of two souls to the same energy field (the kindred): resonating on the same wavelength. Boaz represents the soul's masculine capacity to recognize power and to use it for a higher purpose, to give to others. This recognition nourishes the soul.

After recognizing Ruth as the Moabitess who came back with Naomi, Boaz advises her:

> Go not to glean in another field, neither go from hence, but abide
> here fast by my maidens:
>   Let thine eyes be on the field that they do reap, and go thou after
> them. . . . (Ruth 2:8–9)

These words could be understood as follows: "Do not nurture yourself with the spirit of another, remain focused upon your own experience, your genesis, for it is individual and unique." The passage means that we should be related to our own power. "Gleaning in other fields" illustrates a loss of focus and power in our soul. Psychologically speaking, it is a warning about the inherent danger in projection, the unconscious transfer of our own desires or emotions to another person.

After falling on her face and prostrating herself, Ruth asks Boaz:

Why have I found grace in thine eyes, that thou shouldest take knowledge of me, seeing I am a stranger? (Ruth 2:10)

As we recall, Tamar, Rahab, and Ruth are all strangers who come from foreign lands. The word *stranger* is derived from the Latin word *extraneous,* which begins with ex, the prefix for "out of, outside of our physical body." In this sense, the soul comes from another land, having been exiled from our physical experience, yet it represents the mysterious divine aspect of the personality. Falling to one's face, bowing to the ground: this is the expression of the soul's spirituality anchored in physical reality.

Naomi-Ruth reawakens our awareness of the soul's sacrosanctity in our physical beings. The experience of the soul is earthbound. Harvesting and gleaning intimate the power of transformation in the sacred realm of matter. The transformation takes place in the body, not in the mind. Consciousness of the divine dimension returns through nature, a process known as "the spiritualization of matter."

3. THE NIGHT ON THE THRESHING FLOOR

Naomi makes the following suggestion to Ruth. "[S]hall I not seek rest for thee, that it may be well with thee? And now is not Boaz of our kindred? . . . Behold, he winnoweth barley tonight in the threshing-floor" (Ruth 3:1–2).

Naomi's message to us here is: "Make room for the soul in your life!" But how is that to be accomplished? Naomi's instructions are clear: "Wash thyself therefore, and anoint thee, and put thy raiment upon thee" (Ruth 3:3). Cleanse your soul: return to the source, to the water of life, to your spontaneous, original being, and wash away everything that does not belong to you. Become your true self! Do it with loving care, anoint your soul with life substance, in complete devotion, as you face the divine in yourself! The raiment is the warm embracing divine protection you receive in response to your surrender.

"Winnowing the barley in the threshingfloor" is an act of recognition of what is important in our life, and what is not. The purpose, the core of our life substance has to be released and cleared of all superficial trappings. Only then are we ready to meet, to submit, to integrate, and to make use of the powerful force represented by Boaz.

Naomi instructs Ruth not to make herself known to Boaz until he has finished eating and drinking (Ruth 3:3), after which she should "mark the place where he shall lie, and thou shalt go in . . . and lay thee down; and he will tell thee what thou shalt do" (Ruth 3:4).

Why should Ruth not make herself known to Boaz until he has eaten and drunk? We are being told: "Sustain and nurture your true power, and wait for the right moment to realize it."

> And when Boaz had eaten and drunk, and his heart was merry, he went to lie down at the end of the heap of corn: and she came softly, and uncovered his feet, and laid her down. (Ruth 3:7)

To uncover Boaz's feet means to perceive the physical reality of his power. Boaz is the harvester; he gathers the fruits of his creative labors, demonstrating our potential to bring to maturation the seed of divine love residing in each of us. He represents our capacity to master instinctual impulses and to canalize them in a healthy manner that enhances our physical and psychic sense of well-being. He is the healer and redeemer of the wounds inflicted on our souls.

We are informed that at midnight "the man was afraid, and turned himself: and behold, a woman lay at his feet" (Ruth 3:8). The encounter at midnight takes place on an inner, higher invisible level. It expresses the mystery of the union of two divine forces, male and female. Boaz's moment of fear could be referring to an invisible third presence: the power of love. In a mystical moment we can only humbly surrender and do service: "I am Ruth thine handmaid: spread therefore thy skirt over thine handmaid; for thou art a near kinsman" (Ruth 3:9). ("Spread thy skirt over thine handmaid" was a delicate way to make an offer of marriage.)

Boaz praised Ruth for her kindness and for being focused in her work. When doing the work of the soul, it is important not to be distracted by outer activities, to hold with determination to your path to redemption, even when it is a lonely, hard, and challenging path that calls for faith in yourself and the power of love.

Ruth's complete dedication to her work is honored and rewarded by Boaz's generosity in sending her home to Naomi the following morning with six measures of barley (Ruth 3:15–17). There is a divine law of reciprocity: when we give without expectation of reward, we receive in abundance. But as the story tells us, there is a kinsman more closely related to Ruth than Boaz, and "if he will not do the part of a kinsman to thee, than I will do the part of a kinsman to thee" (Ruth 3:13). The unnamed kinsman represents an obstacle that has to be overcome before the unification of the male and female forces.

4. THE WEDDING OF RUTH AND BOAZ

Then went Boaz up to the gate, and sat him down there: and, behold, the kinsman of whom Boaz spake came by; unto whom he said, Ho, such a one! turn aside, sit down here. And he turned aside, and sat down. (Ruth 4:1)

To redeem our soul, we have to go back to the source where the Goddess ". . . was the image of the Whole, when life emerged from and returned to her, and when she was conceived as the door or gateway to a hidden dimension of being that was her womb, the eternal source and regenerator of life."[4] In this way we get in touch with the power of that indestructible life force that the four biblical women carry. But this source, as we well know, has been buried beneath layers of patriarchal belief systems, represented by the nameless kinsman who refuses to redeem Ruth because he would damage his patrimony—in other words, his patriarchal world (Ruth 4:6).

It is noteworthy that in the past, "matrimony" meant the equivalent of "patrimony," but with the inheritance of property being determined by maternal line of descent. The word *marriage* was derived from the Latin *maritare,* meaning "union under the auspices of the Goddess Aphrodite-Mari."[5] In this light Boaz is redeeming the inheritance of the Goddess's values, and thereby redeeming her lost image. Naomi-Ruth-Orpah have opened the divine gate by bringing to consciousness the perpetual connection to the source of all life.

> Moreover Ruth the Moabitess, the wife of Mahlon, I have purchased to be my wife, to raise up the name of the dead upon his inheritance, that the name of the dead not be cut off from among his brethren, and from the gate of his place: ye are witnesses this day. (Ruth 4:10)

This passage clearly refers to not being cut off or separated "from the gate of his place," that is, from the hidden dimension of the feminine source of life.

Dealing with the kinsman in the presence of the elders of the city (Ruth 4:2) indicates the necessity of standing witness to the redemption of the soul, providing evidence of it. What the elders "see" is proof of the eternal continuity of life in Boaz's masculine and feminine aspect, as the *one* source of life.

> And all the people that were in the gate, and the elders, said, We are witnesses. The Lord make the woman that is come into thine house like Rachel and like Leah, which two did build the house of Israel. . . .
>
> And let thy house be like the house of Pharez, whom Tamar bare unto Judah, of the seed which the Lord shall give thee of this young woman. (Ruth 4:11–12)

The feminine line is honored as the builder of the house of Israel. Baring and Cashford state in their commentary on the evolution of Yahweh:

Israel figures in the imagery as the earthly bride of Yahweh. . . .

But from our knowledge of other cultures we can say that the *relation* of masculine to feminine, as expressed in the sacred marriage of goddess and god, or god and goddess (depending on the culture), was always the culmination of a religious ritual. And this must tell us something about a universal need to reconcile these two polarities of human experience . . . the divine image of the masculine principle requires a complementary divine image of the feminine principle if the image of divinity is to inspire and heal. The Ethical Word of the Law and the Loving Compassion of the Heart may not have to be represented as divine figures—as god and goddess—as long as both conceptions and principles are present in the divine image. The archetypal masculine quality of Transcendence and the archetypal feminine quality of Immanence may both be necessary in the image of divinity for the sacred marriage to take place in the human soul.[6]

The principles of the "Loving Compassion of the Heart" and the "Ethical Word of the Law" are clearly expressed in the figures of Naomi-Ruth and Boaz. They provide the criteria—the qualities of transcendence and immanence—that enable the sacred marriage in our souls to eventuate. Spirit and matter are present and become one. Tamar and Judah are referred to as having initiated this unifying process: "And let thy house be like the house of Pharez, whom Tamar bore unto Judah . . ." (Ruth 4:12).

So Boaz took Ruth, and she was his wife: and when he went in unto her, the Lord gave her conception, and she bare a son.

And the women said unto Naomi, Blessed be the Lord, which hath not left thee this day without a kinsman, that his name may be famous in Israel.

And he shall be unto thee a restorer of thy life, and a nourisher of thine old age: for thy daughter-in-law, which loveth thee, which is better to thee than seven sons, hath born him.

And Naomi took the child, and laid it in her bosom, and became nurse unto it.

And the women her neighbours gave it a name, saying, There is a son born to Naomi; and they called his name Obed: he is the father of Jesse, the father of David. (Ruth 4:13–18)

The child is called Obed, that is, "restorer of life" (*meshiv nefesh*), which can be literally translated as "returner of the soul."[7] This is most significant. In the mystery of divine conception, the soul returns to the home of the heart and is nourished with unconditional love. The newborn consciousness (Obed) submits to, and serves, a higher power.

As I wrote the words "returner of the soul," a beautiful, iridescent butterfly (a symbol of the soul), very unusual for the time of year, fluttered in and came to rest on my windowsill—a synchronistic message from the invisible world! It evoked in me a profound feeling of gratitude and the sensation that I was holding Ruth's child in my lap, meeting the divine in myself and realizing: "The body is the home of the soul!"

If Ruth is considered better than seven sons, then she is related to the number eight, which is an ancient symbol of eternity. There are mystical events in life in which the presence of the soul is experienced by stepping into eternity. It is a state of suspension between time and space wherein all the events in life merge together in one motionless, eternal moment. You feel that everything in your life has yearned for this unique moment, has starved for it. Everything falls into place. You know with consummate clarity the meaning of your destiny. The purpose of your whole life has been to experience this eternal moment, to surrender to the overwhelming, divine embrace.

EIGHT

Bathsheba

The Unfinished Story of the Daughter of the Goddess

The story of Bathsheba—told in Samuel 11:1–27 and 12:1–31 and I Kings 1:1–31 and I Kings 2:13–23—is like the negative of a photograph that has not yet been developed. There are very few mentions of Bathsheba in the Bible. In the genealogy of Jesus, she appears merely as "Uriah's wife," and she is the only one of our four Old Testament women who is not mentioned there by name. Bathsheba's story conveys a sense of incompleteness, for it has been cleansed of embarrassing truths in the course of translations and interpretations. But her name is most revealing: in Hebrew, *Bat-scheba* means "daughter of abundance." Sheba is also a mythical queen who came to visit Solomon, the son of Bathsheba (I Kings 10:1–3).

Bath means "daughter," and sheba means "seven." The name *Zenobia* in Aramaic means "daughter of the Goddess." The famous queen Zenobia Septima was the "seventh Bathsheba."[1] This seems to indicate that Bathsheba is the hidden daughter of the Goddess. This might explain why she is merely mentioned in passing as the "wife of Uriah" and why we hear so little of her. Nonetheless, the indestructible life force emerges again in her person.

As we have seen, David slept with Bathsheba even though he knew that she was Uriah's wife. After she let him know that she had conceived, David then called Uriah home from war, and tried to send him to his wife: "Go down to thy house, and wash thy feet" (II Samuel 11:8). Uriah, however, did not go, but rather slept at the door of the king's house. Even when David gave him food and drink, he did not go to his house and wife, thus making it impossible to claim that the child was his. David then sent Uriah to the front so that he would be killed in battle.

> And when the wife of Uriah heard that Uriah her husband was dead, she mourned for her husband.
>
> And when the mourning was past, David sent and fetched her to his house, and she became his wife, and bare him a son. But the thing that David had done displeased the Lord. (II Samuel 11:26–27)

David was growing old and losing his strength, and he stayed home in Jerusalem because he was weary of war. In the springtime, kings went forth to battle, for it was the time when the old king had to make way for a renewal, for a new image of the divine—a cyclic, natural change. It is comparable to our times, which come at the end of a great cycle, when everything is pointing to the urge to change and transform our belief systems, to enlarge our consciousness. The story of Bathsheba provides us with important intimations about how to make the step upward, to a higher level of comprehension and awareness. Everything is moving toward purification and the potential evolution of the old image of the Goddess through her daughter, just as the old king David has to make way for a renewal in the form of his future son, Solomon.

David saw Bathsheba washing herself, and in the following passage, we learn that she was "purified from her uncleanness" (II Samuel 11:2, 4). This refers to her monthly cycle, symbolizing her blood bond to the great Mother Goddess. Here the thread that connects the other three women becomes menstrual blood: the lunar image of the Goddess emerges in physical reality as an underlying spiritual potential to incarnate in a daughter, to become an experienced reality in the collective consciousness. The feminists have done pioneering work on behalf of this process of maturing consciousness, but have not yet brought it to completion, as they have not come to terms with the masculine divine image.

Another potential meaning of the biblical image is that in the eyes of the established patriarchal consciousness of that age, the feminine divine could emerge on a physical level only as impurity. Today, this outlook lives on, as modern science formulates methods to suppress menstruation—a means for silencing the body. This is precisely what happened to the image of Mary in our Christian tradition. She has been cleansed of any impurity, of all that is held to be a sin or evil.

The menstrual cycle is also associated with the number seven, which is an inherent part of Bathsheba's name. Seven is a holy number of completeness, abundance, and achievement. As we have seen, seven contains three and four, symbolizing the unity of masculine and feminine. Seven in this context might be intimating the necessity for a reinstatement of the Goddess's image in her daughter Bathsheba, thus initiating a new life cycle of greater understanding of her power. Bathsheba's ablutions would then convey the meaning of freeing oneself from all the traditional roles to which women are consigned.

In this way Bathsheba represents that feminine power able to transcend all roles, because she has incorporated all of them. She is that mysterious force that has gone through myriad transformations and is now able to recognize the One and to be a part of it, without losing herself in it. She is also the conciliation of inner experience with outer concrete reality. Bathsheba represents the capacity for transformation, for becoming fertile, able to give form to a new way of life. When David glimpsed that power, he was seduced by it.

At the same time, David's actions could also be viewed as representing impatience, the inability to wait for things to evolve in the natural course of the cycle of time. The masculine (in both genders) wants to accelerate time, and that is the reason why things ended badly in the story of Bathsheba.

Even today, this problem represents one of the greatest dangers of our modern world. There is an abyss between technical and scientific progress, and the way of the soul. We have no time to make room for spiritual growth in our lives, nor do we respect cyclical growth in nature. We may have made enormous strides technically and scientifically, but our ethics seem to have remained trapped in those of the Iron Age. The only things that have changed are the forms the barbarism and cruelty take. In their subchapter "War as the Ethos of the Iron Age," Baring and Cashford state:

> The Iron Age is dominated by a mythology of war, in which the hero is seen politically as the mighty warrior. The ideal of the king was no longer to be the shepherd of his people, as it was in early Sumeria, but the mighty conqueror. . . . Cruelty became a virtue and barbarism a way of life.[2]

David began as a shepherd, only to become a mighty warrior and king. Many factors in the story indicate that he was tiring of these roles and felt the winds of change when he met Bathsheba. His act of adultery and sending Uriah to his death constitute an effort to change and transform the old image of the divine warrior king. The word *adultery* comes from the Latin *adulterare,* which means to alter something, to break an old pattern. Uriah the Hittite can be regarded as the warrior aspect of David's personality (the Hittites were a clan of warriors). Washing the feet means putting oneself in the service of love. We might thus conclude that Uriah did not want to change: he served war not love. He represents a masculine element clinging to its warrior role, unwilling to change its standpoint. David's sin was therefore his inability to transform and integrate his warrior nature. Instead, he just killed it off—and this is what "displeased the Lord" (II Samuel 11:27). The prophet Nathan says to David:

> [T]hou hast killed Uriah the Hittite with the sword . . . and hast slain him with the sword of the children of Ammon.
>
> Now therefore the sword shall never depart from thine house; because thou hast despised me, and hast taken the wife of Uriah the Hittite to be thy wife. (II Samuel 12:9–10)

In other words, because the energy invested in the primitive identification with warrior was not transformed and integrated on a conscious level, and since we cannot just "kill off" psychic energy (as the findings of depth psychology have demonstrated), it continued to function as a repressed content in David's unconscious, ultimately to visit violence, rape, death, and incest on his family.

Is this not a reality that still permeates our modern world, along with war and destruction, as a result of the failure to integrate the warrior archetype?

Bathsheba mourned for her husband. Such an expression of grief is an elaboration, acceptance, and integration of loss. As she had been married to Uriah, who embodied David's warrior nature, what would her mourning signify? We might understand this as follows: being the wife of a warrior, she is nameless, she has not been given an identity: that is, she is unconscious. She is not named until she has come to the attention of, and been recognized by, the king, the ordering principle in the psyche. Integrating the warrior archetype also involves the discovery of a powerful feminine creative force in the psyche, associated with the cyclic renewal of the life of the soul.

Even though David "lay with" Bathsheba, he had not truly integrated his warrior aspect. His attempt failed, as is illustrated by the illness and ultimate death of his child by "Uriah's wife." We are told that for seven days, David fasted and lay upon the earth all night long—but to no avail, for the child died.

> Then David arose from the earth, and washed, and anointed himself,
> and changed his apparel, and came into the house of the Lord and
> worshipped. . . . (II Samuel 12:20)

What kind of message does this image convey? Fasting is a method
for invoking the divine; lying all night upon the earth evokes images
from the age-old belief that new life is born from the earth and of the
motif of the eternal return. Psychologically speaking, the king represents a masculine principle of law and order, which, in the best of
worlds, is also in touch with Mother Earth, heeding her wise counsel
and building a relationship with her. The advice is the same as that
given by Naomi to Ruth to wash and anoint herself and put her raiment
on. In other words, change your attitude toward life to one of total surrender to your soul. Honor both universal divine parents, Mother and
Father, restore the lost harmony between them, between the inner and
outer worlds. Then the opportunity will arise to ignite anew the fire of
creativity, to transform destructive aggressiveness into a new form of
life in which peace and wisdom prevail.

The following lines confirm this interpretation:

> And David comforted Bathsheba his wife, and went in unto her, and
> lay with her: and she bare a son, and he called his name Solomon:
> and the Lord loved him. (II Samuel 12:24)

It is interesting to note that Bathsheba is mentioned here for the
first time by name as David's wife, as a sign of her newly acquired
identity through David's change of consciousness. In Hebrew, *Solomon*
means "peaceful," and his wisdom became legendary.

Bathsheba, the queen, attempts the important task of resur-
recting the lost harmony. She embodies the profound knowledge of
the deepest truth, in our innermost being, of who we are. She is in
touch with divine law, she knows of the weaving of human destiny,

she mediates between the divine and the human. She comes alive in our physical bodies as a potent energy that reminds us that we are part of the substance of the Goddess; we partake of her immanence.

Bathsheba's knowledge is deeply rooted in the experience and wisdom she has achieved through the realization of the other three women as a vital, inseparable part of herself. It is this greater vision that endows her with such abundance and completeness. As queen she reflects boundless divine love, and her actions in the outer world are an expression of the sacred law of reciprocity: "As in Heaven, so on Earth." Bathsheba embodies this spiritual potential in the soul, which yearns to be recognized and to incarnate in our inner and outer lives. When this potential is fully realized, she becomes the daughter of the eternal Mother. She is experienced as the divine in feminine form. But, sadly, this is not what happened in Bathsheba's story.

David had another son, Adonijah, who was ambitious and proclaimed himself king in an attempt to usurp David's throne. When this news reached the ears of Nathan the prophet, he advised Bathsheba to save her own life and that of her son Solomon by reminding David of his promise to make Solomon his successor. Nathan suggested she ask David to explain why Adonijah had ascended to the throne. Nathan also promised that he would follow her into David's presence and confirm her testimony. Bathsheba followed Nathan's instructions; after having heard her out, David assured her ". . . Solomon thy son shall reign after me, and he shall sit upon my throne in my stead . . . Then Bathsheba bowed with her face to the earth, and did reverence to the king, and said, Let my lord king David live forever" (I Kings 1:30–31).

The name *Adonijah* is of interest, for it means "my God is Yahweh." If we approach this firstborn son as another facet of David's character, he would then be David's ambitious side, his shadow, which wants to usurp the throne—in a certain sense, to overshadow the king's power. In this light, Adonijah may be understood as a rigid attitude faithful to the old image of the Yahweh who says of himself ". . . I am

Alpha and Omega, the beginning and the end, the first and the last (Revelation 22:13) ". . . there is none beside me. I am the Lord and there is none else" (Isaiah 45:6). This is an intransigent God who is to be recognized in our own inflexibility: "No opinion is allowed except my own!" Adonijah blocks the process of evolution, holding back the energy of transformation by being too tied to the tradition of fear of the unknown.

Nathan, the prophet, representing the one who carries the relationship to divine intent, recognized the danger threatening the lives of Bathsheba and Solomon. Solomon is the bearer of the divine seed, chosen to be ancestor to Jesus. He is the symbol of a newly emergent identity of the divine image, a new configuration in our soul, which is the fruit of the conjunction of opposites through the sacred marriage of feminine and masculine, of king and queen. This nascent formation is always in danger of being overruled by collective forces serving egotistical goals.

In the process of transformation and evolution it is inevitably the feminine that opens the door to a new understanding, for it stands in natural relation to the cyclic renewal of life and to changes within the soul. This link is created through the unifying force of love, incarnated in Bathsheba, for she used her power in the interest of love, to ensure that Solomon would be given David's throne. Solomon, the new king, symbolizes a new level of consciousness in us, which needs the feminine power in order to become a discerning and wise ruling center in our soul.

At a later point in the story, Solomon has a dream in which he asks God to bequeath wisdom to him:

Give therefore thy servant an understanding heart to judge thy people, that I may discern between good and bad. . . . (I Kings 3:9)

These lines, in their simplicity and essentiality, capture the wisdom that unites heart and mind. While writing them down, I had the realization that I had been interpreting the dynamic embodied in the person of Adonijah without the understanding of the heart. I felt blocked in the writing process, as I was not regarding him in his wholeness. In fact, his faithfulness and attachment to tradition is an important and vital force in the evolution of the divine image. It is the indispensable link to the past: the memory of sacred contents of long-established masculine traditions, which must be integrated with loving care into the expanded consciousness. Yet, as the story reveals, this integration was not realized, for in a sense, in killing Adonijah, Solomon repeated David's pattern.

After David's death, Adonijah approaches Bathsheba, asking her to intervene on his behalf with her son Solomon. Adonijah desires Solomon's permission to marry Abishag, a fair young virgin who had cherished the old king David because "he gat no heat . . . and let her cherish him, and let her lie in thy bosom, that my lord the king may get heat" (I Kings 1:1–2).

Why does Adonijah now wish to marry Abishag? If he is taken as representing the devoted memory of sacred traditions of the past, he needs the virginal aspect of the soul, his inner feminine heritage, in order to be integrated into consciousness. Marriage is, in a psychological sense, the unification of unconscious content with consciousness. The warmth of the heart makes it possible to resurrect lost memories of things past, in a manner that relates them to the present. The result is a more objective view of things in their totality.

When Bathsheba went to King Solomon to speak on behalf of Adonijah "he rose up to meet her, and bowed himself unto her, and sat down on his throne, and caused a seat to be set for the king's mother; and she sat on his right hand" (I Kings 2:19). In those times, the throne of the king represented Yahweh's ownership over Jerusalem and his chosen people. Solomon's symbolic gesture therefore mirrors an intent to honor Bathsheba as the hidden divine feminine aspect of Yahweh, as an active principle (the right hand) of God, partaking of his power. To be placed on the right-hand side of

God was a great privilege. We could understand this as a movement in the collective psyche of that era to reestablish the original order in which Wisdom (Sophia) stood alongside God from the beginning.

Bathsheba then said to David:

> I desire one small petition of thee; I pray thee, say me not nay. And the king said unto her, Ask on, my mother: for I will not say thee nay.
>
> And she said, Let Abishag the Shunammite be given to Adonijah thy brother to wife. (I Kings 2:20–21)

Solomon was enraged and asked her why not "ask for him the kingdom also; for he is mine elder brother" (I Kings 2:22). Solomon then proceeded to have Adonijah put to death that very day.

The killing of Adonijah is reminiscent of the story of Uriah's death. Solomon failed to realize his chance to integrate the conservative tendency in human nature through union with the feminine principle. Solomon's initial reaction, a promise not to deny Bathsheba's petition, was a spontaneous response from the heart. Unfortunately, his second reaction, after hearing the content of Bathsheba's request, was triggered by his fear of losing power. This denotes a split between heart and mind! At this point, Bathsheba disappears from the story and a tremendous potential to incarnate as a daughter of the Goddess (as her name suggests) departs with her, becoming lost to living memory.

It is from this perspective that we might regard Solomon's encounter with the queen of Sheba—namely, that the feminine principle of the daughter has regressed and vanished, although it did eventually reemerge as the Mother Goddess in the image of the queen of Sheba.

Although Solomon's mother Bathsheba did manage to instill in him a connection to the Mother Goddess, the image of Bathsheba has been denuded of its power. She is defeated in the biblical story. We are left with a sense of incompleteness. Her feminine wisdom was not integrated into the collective soul of that period, but rather was split off, taking the form of the many wives of Solomon. In the case of these wives, a fourfold process such as we see in our four biblical women—who are the carriers of the sacred seed of evolution of the divine feminine image—is less evident.

Bathsheba, as the daughter of the Goddess, differs from a Mother Goddess such as Asherah, who was worshipped by the Canaanites. The Daughter Goddess, as von Franz points out, is nearer to humanity than is the Mother Goddess, just as God the Father is further away from humankind than is Christ. She is the expression of the capacity to view the process of transformation from a distance and the ability to contemplate the past with gentleness and compassion. This emotional objectivity is that "understanding heart to judge [and] discern between good and bad" (I Kings 3:9) that Solomon prayed for.

The daughter sees things as they really are, without projections. She enables us to experience the wholeness of nature and spirit, heart and mind, because she has herself suffered through the laceration of the opposites. Although Bathsheba vanished from the biblical story, the daughter of the Goddess, whom she represents, has not vanished from our hearts. We rediscover her in our tie to divine intent, when we open our souls to its voice, which allows the holy seed to flourish and express itself in unconditional love.

She is the door to Mary.

As daughters of the Goddess, we are called to complete the unfinished story.

PART THREE

---◄◉►---

The Conception of Mary

A Symbolic Interpretation
of the Apocryphal Legend

---◄◉►---

M Y JOURNEY BEGAN WITH THE DOGMA of the Immaculate Conception and it ends with the legend of the nativity of Mary, yet in their essence they are one.

In my pilgrimage, both outward and homeward bound, I descended into the depths of the past, and at the same time made a leap into the future. Along the way, I learned how the cultural images imprinted in our consciousness and unconscious differ from the deeper ones buried and forgotten in our soul. Slowly the voice of the exiled soul grew stronger and gained authority, even as I surrendered to my own experiences. Experiences are always individual, but when they penetrate into the realm of transpersonal events, they become coupled with universal powers through which we learn to rediscover the relation between humankind and the divine.

Those powers grant us the courage to cut through old belief systems and long established patterns of thought and to bring to light the hidden treasures that long to be unearthed. They help free the way of resentment and anger so that we can learn to sense the presence of an unknown higher truth. This higher truth is the power that wants to restore the lost harmony and completeness in our souls through introducing the missing daughter into the holy family.

After many years of research, I came to the conclusion that the Immaculate Conception is the "architect's blueprint" and the nativity of Mary is the realization of that divine design, its incarnation in human beings and the personification of the image of the divine daughter.

The four biblical women are signposts to the unfolding of this hidden pattern and design, whose intention it is to beget a new consciousness differentiated from that shaped by the old image of the Mother Goddess. We have seen that this was the ultimate goal in the story of Bathsheba, who we identified as the daughter ("Bath") of the Goddess. This attempt was, however, abortive; in the encounter with King Solomon, it ended in a regression to the image of the queen of Sheba (the Mother Goddess). Furthermore, Bathsheba became Solomon's mother and her daughter aspect remained merely a matter of her name.

In Christianity, God the Father incarnated in the Son, which, as von Franz notes, was a "tremendous religious collective experience." She writes:

> The same tendency can be seen in the development of the antique mother goddess who wants to incarnate in a human daughter, but the impulse remains abortive. It has nowhere been carried through and become a religious event. The cult of the mother goddess got stuck and suppressed and then reappeared later in the cult of the Virgin Mary, but with great mental reservations and precautions for the disinfection of her dark aspect.[1]

We see the same phenomenon in the dogma of the Immaculate Conception, in which it is not the daughter of the Goddess but rather the future mother of Jesus Christ who is untainted by original sin.

The divine daughter is a new, differentiated image of the eternal Mother. She represents the principle of the integration of opposites, as we saw in the unfinished story of Bathsheba—a principle that has not been recognized. She represents the ability of the feminine principle in the soul to harmonize dualities such as father and mother, light and dark, life and death, human and divine, spirit and matter, thereby creating a new consciousness that transcends dualistic thinking even as it encompasses it.

This, in my opinion, is the deeper meaning behind the designation of Mary as being exempt from original sin. It might well be the meaning behind the new emerging feminine spirit: Mary in the New Testament, grasped in her wholeness, is the incarnation of the oneness of the four Old Testament women who preceded her. The fifth is the quintessence of the four, the distillation of their true essence. Mary is thus the center, she is all of them and none of them. She no longer needs to play a specific role because all of them are embraced in her nature. She represents simultaneously both the independence of the soul and the willing subjection to divine will.

It is most important to acknowledge the fact that the incarnation of the divine daughter in a human being involves, transforms, and evolves the image of the Mother Goddess as well. In this process, she becomes the original matrix of Christian consciousness. In the final instance, this is the experience of God's presence as Son and the experience, through Mary, of the Great Mother's presence as Daughter, which reveals the underlying totality of the divine.

Let us now look at the actual legend of Mary's nativity. There are two versions in the Apocryphal gospels; one (*I Vangeli apocrifi*) is attributed to James, a supposed brother of Jesus, and the other (*Vangeli apocrifi Natività e infanzia*) to a pseudo-Matthew. A third version is found in *Die Legenda Aurea,* written by a bishop, Jacobus de Voragine, in about 1292 in Genoa, Italy. Since each of these narratives has been carefully scrutinized and sifted for accuracy by scholars, I have taken the liberty of drawing on all three versions for pertinent source material that is not found in the others.

◄o►

NINE

The Parents of Mary

Joachim was a rich and pious Hebrew from the tribe of Judah. He married Anna of Bethlehem, who also belonged to the tribe of Judah. They divided their wealth into three parts: one they gave to the temple and the servant, one they gave to pilgrims and the poor, and one they kept for themselves. Yet after twenty years had passed in this way, they were still childless. They therefore gave God their word that should He fulfill their wish, they would consecrate their child to Him.

For this purpose, they went to Jerusalem to make an offering in the temple. However, Joachim was ordered to leave the temple as being unworthy to make offerings to the Lord of the Law: being without offspring, he was held to be in a state of disgrace. Stricken with grief, he did not return to his wife, but retired into the desert, where he fasted for forty days and forty nights.

The lesson here is that we have to go through the flesh to reach the spirit—that is, through the humanness of Joachim and Anna. They express a creative process in the soul that is experienced and realized in an interaction between the inner and outer worlds, between spirit and matter. To come from the same tribe, to share the same roots, means that the eternal thread of life's continuity in its feminine and masculine expression strives for integration in consciousness as one. This attempt at integration is rejected by the official religious system—which itself is the cause of the sterility.

The sharing of the wealth by dividing it into three parts suggests that in the course of a creative process or evolution of consciousness, we have to perceive, nurture, and honor three levels of consciousness: the spiritual, soul, and matter. One portion goes to the spirit (the temple), another to the soul (the pilgrims and the poor), and the third to sustain material existence.

When we read that after twenty years, Joachim and Anna were still childless, what is in fact being expressed is a complete split, a condition in which the opposite—of inner and outer, spirit and matter—are acutely polarized.

How different is the situation today? The official religious system clearly rejects the integration of masculine and feminine consciousness; there is considerable disharmony between spirit, soul, and matter in our modern world, where the focus is usually on material existence; and we are witnessing polarization of many kinds, such as, for instance, in climatic changes and extremes. We are living in an extremely critical period of great conflicts and transformations. Yet there is also cause for great hope, as so many prophecies foretell, for a new consciousness to be born in our souls.

In the Old Testament the affliction of sterility is also the sign of impending miraculous birth. In *Die Legenda Aurea,* we read that when God closes a woman's womb, he does so solely for the reason—which we recognize only after the fact—that the child to come is a divine gift, as was the case with Sarah and Isaac, Rachel and Joseph, and Hannah and Samuel.

Joachim and Anna's consecration of their child to God can be understood to mean that every aspect of creativity is sacred: it does not belong to us but rather is consecrated to the divine. We have to become conscious of the miraculous, sacred aspect inherent in every creative process, be it a child of the flesh, the soul, or the spirit.

According to the legend, Joachim withdrew into the desert to fast for forty days and nights. The desert is a place of introspection and solitude, but also of fear, temptation, and facing up to outworn life patterns that have lost their vitality and purposiveness and need to be transformed. The desert is an environment of extremes, one where the power of nature can be frightening and inexorable. Yet, at the same time, it is a place where sorrow and pain are healed, where we are given the opportunity to experience grace in being touched by the divine, to encounter our true unadorned self and to shed our old skin, to break antiquated laws. It is a space of coming "face to face" with oneself. In the Bible, forty is the number associated with expectation, preparation, and completion. In the lives of human beings, it is often linked with coming up against individual destiny and questioning the meaning of life, which is the door opening onto awareness of the divine intent underlying our lives.

> While Joachim was in the desert, Anna was weeping over the loss of her husband and her sterility. Her servant Judith said to her "How long will your soul remain oppressed? On the great day of the Lord, you should not be sorrowful. Take this headband, which was given to me by the mistress of the laboratory. I am not allowed to wear it, because I am a servant and it bears the royal seal."
>
> Anna, however, refused to accept the band on the grounds that she had never done such things and that God had already humiliated her enough. She told Judith to leave, saying "Mayhap it was given to you by one who seduced you, and you came here to make me an accomplice in your transgression."
>
> Judith replied "What kind of curse can I put on you when God has closed your womb?"

The dialogue between the two women is cryptic and highly intriguing. The name Judith comes from the Hebrew *jadah,* "to praise." Judith was probably a servant of the Great Goddess, whom she praised and celebrated. Judith would thus represent the force in the soul that helps us to overcome sorrow and pain, transforming emotional helplessness, delusions, and bitterness into love and wisdom.

I can find no explanation for the term used in the *Vangeli apocrifi Natività e infanzia,* which I have translated as "laboratory;" I can only conjecture that it has to do with "labor," "work," or possibly the realm of transformation, as in alchemy. The headband with the royal insignia, which calls to mind a queen's crown, given to Judith by the "mistress of the laboratory," may be an image of the loving power that masters and dominates emotional distress, which is linked with labor, with work. By means of this headband bearing the token of royalty, Judith is reminding Anna of the latter's royal-divine descent, which lends her the inherent capacity to create new forms of life, to carry the divine seed.

As we have seen, Anna's name points to the Great Mother Anna, she whom the Romans referred to as "Eternal Anna," mother of the Aeons. She appears at the end of the Old Testament and at the beginning of the New Testament. She represents the threshold, the door opening on to a new understanding of that which is hidden, occult, and buried, as the Greek term *apocrifon* means. In the legend, it is difficult to recognize, behind Anna's sorrow, the powerful force that wants to incarnate in a daughter.

Why did Anna refuse the help offered by her servant Judith, even accusing her of an attempt to implicate her, Anna, in Judith's transgression? And who might the seducer she refers to be? We have to give thought once again to the many translations these legends have undergone.

In *Die Legenda Aurea,* there is no reference to the servant Judith, and in *Vangeli apocrifi Natività e infanzia,* we read that this text is most likely no longer intact: "It is probable that the clarity of the story has been diminished by the omission of narrative elements that appeared in the original text." The expurgations are of heretical passages, one of which might be that Anna *accepted* the headband offered to her by Judith because in her person she recognized the servant of the Divine

Mother. Anna would then have been "seduced" by the gift. If we proceed from this assumption, everything else falls into place.

We are told that Anna took off her mourning garments, washed and anointed her hair, donned her wedding dress, and went out into the garden. These actions mirror a complete reversal of attitude, the possibility of a new identity through her daughter—a transformation of old thought patterns and images, expressing her full power in a new setting, after it had been excluded for so very long. Anna's wedding dress symbolizes union with a new aspect in life: giving oneself over to it and becoming a part of it. It means that a long repressed aspect is to be included, at last, in consciousness.

The legend goes on to relate that Anna sits beneath a laurel tree in which she discovers a sparrow's nest. She embarks on a lengthy lament, in which she asks who conceived and gave birth to her, for she has been engendered as a malediction in the eyes of the children of Israel; she has been outraged, mocked, and expelled from the temple of the Lord. She asks in whose likeness she has been created, for in contrast to her, everything else on earth—the birds, the animals, the waters, the earth itself—is fruitful and blessed of God.

It is not difficult to recognize in Anna's lament the grieving of the repressed, expelled Great Mother over the loss of relationship with her and her creation. The motif of sitting under the laurel tree speaks to us of her eternal, cosmic being, representing the indestructible life force in our soul.

At this point in the legend, an angel, God's messenger, reveals himself both to Joachim and to Anna, announcing that their prayers will be answered and that Anna will conceive a child. The angel informs them independently that this revelation will be confirmed when they reunite by the golden door of Jerusalem.

Angels are manifestations of the love that the divine holds for us humans; in their revelations they communicate the divine plan that guides and protects us as we traverse our earthly path.

Joachim represents our capacity to recognize divine intent, while

Anna is our inner ability to realize the divine design by bringing it down to earth, by grounding it in this reality. Together they reestablish the lost harmony through love. The principle of life, Mary, is engendered by two opposites, which need to be in equilibrium; then, and only then, does Mary become the mother of the incarnated spirit. *When we overcome duality, the matrix becomes virgin.*

The golden door is the incorruptible, virginal place in our human soul, which is a reflection of the world soul, the *anima mundi*, the immanent cause or principle of life, order, consciousness, and self-awareness in the physical world. On a cosmic level, Anna Perenna, Mother of Aeons, conceives a new *Zeitalter*, a new age. In this sense, Anna is the golden door to a cosmic consciousness, which allows us to recognize our interdependence with all of creation. James Hillman writes, "The grandmother of Jesus, St. Anne, older than Mary, Queen of Heaven, has as her emblem a door."[1]

But how are we to envision the way in which all that is signified by Mary's foremothers is brought together in her? I like to imagine them as four energy streams flowing from the same source, like the four rivers mentioned in Genesis 2:10: ". . . and a river went out of Eden to water the garden: and from thence it was parted into four heads." They are four indestructible life forces coming alive in us at certain stations of our life and "watering" our souls to help us grow spiritually and finally return to the one source on a higher level of consciousness.

Tamar gives us the inspiration, the longing to search for the lost wholeness with commitment.

Rahab sets free our identity, gifting us with the strength and power we need to fight along the path.

Ruth offers the enduring loyalty, trust, and love needed to accomplish the task.

Bathsheba provides the courage to act with the wisdom and the knowledge garnered along the way, in harmonic relation with the inner vision.

In Mary, all these energies are molded together into a new consciousness to become *light*. This light embraces the visible and the invisible world, matter and spirit as one to become Mary-Sophia. This new consciousness is the ability to view things from an eternal perspective without losing our grounding in this world (as the motif of Anna sitting beneath a laurel tree suggests), thereby creating a permanent connection to the divine.

Recognition of the divine in ourselves enables us to see the divine in others. We then meet one another by the "golden door to Jerusalem" in unconditional love, as humble human beings. This is the moment when we begin to learn to reflect on, and to act in accordance with, divine will and love, as Mary did.

When announcing the birth of her *daughter,* Anna exclaims: "Today my soul has been magnified!"

I am writing these concluding lines on the eighth of December, the feast day of the Immaculate Conception, the celebration of the conception and birth of *Marianic consciousness,* which holds, at its heart, the divine seed of Christ.

A life cycle of many years has come to a close, and a new one is emerging.

Mary Magdalene— The Soul-Teacher

in the

New Testament

Addition and Completion to

Feminine Mysteries in the Bible

The last lines in chapter eight were: "A life cycle of many years has come to a close and a new one is emerging."

When I wrote those words seven years ago, I didn't know how true they would become, not only on a personal level but on a collective level as well. But there is still an inner voice asking: Who is Mary? Why has the aspect of the daughter been neglected in Christianity in favor of the Virgin Mother aspect?

An answer comes up: Because she would have become too great a challenge to the patriarchal world. A daughter presupposes a Divine Mother; she mirrors the continuity of the feminine indestructible life force emerging again in consciousness. She signifies, as sustained in Gnostic teaching, "that any concept of duality of Mother and Father, or a Trinity of Mother, Father, and Son has to be extended to a quaternity that includes a Daughter, who is the bride of the Son and the Mother of the next level of creation."[1]

As discussed at the beginning of this work, quaternity is the expression of wholeness. The completed sacred family gives us the possibility of living the totality of human experience in four divine images. Through the stories of the four Old Testament women, we have followed the struggle of the daughter archetype to incarnate in consciousness, which is still missing. It reflects how difficult it is to let go of the old image of the Mother Goddess and give space and life to a consciousness that goes beyond conditional love and ego.

A good example of this problem is the current tendency in Italy, which is vividly discussed in the media, for young men of thirty or more to continue living at home or coming back to their mothers, because it's more convenient and cheaper, and because *Di mamma c'è ne una sola!*—"A mother there is only one!" The Gnostic myth of Sophia personifies the human soul as the daughter of the Great Mother. So in this sense, men have to redeem the soul as daughter still projected in the *mamma*. It mirrors the defeat of the male to grow up and develop independent and mature feelings.

The church doesn't want a rejuvenation of the image of the mother of Christ and has long repressed the figure of the daughter, but now a powerful breakthrough of the other face of the mother archetype is taking place, incorporated by another Mary: Mary Magdalene or Miriam, bride and companion of Christ, his female side, who is love made visible.

Through a revelation of the Archangel Uriel we are informed that Mary Magdalene had a daughter, Sara* (which means "princess"), who was also conceived through the Holy Spirit. She represents, we are told, the supernatural event taking place after the Son of God has departed; she is intentionally of feminine gender. The Holy Spirit was infused in the body of Miriam and once again female sexuality became the elec-

---

*Margaret Starbird in *The Woman with the Alabaster Jar* (1993) proclaimed that Mary had a daughter named Sara.

tive vehicle of the divine. This is the great secret that has always been hidden, we are told by the Archangel Uriel.[2]

Mary Magdalene entered my life after I had realized deep inside that my life work was not quite complete. To finish my task I had to go through the hardest test in my life, a dark night of the soul. During this difficult time I didn't grasp the reason for the suffering. I felt abandoned on a dark sea, a symbol of the unconscious.

At a certain point in my journey I ceased to struggle against it and I let go of myself, trusting that something was happening inside that would manifest in due time. I was guided by Thomas Moore's words: "Everything depends on how the dark night is handled: will you try to overcome it and run away from it, or will you let it transform you and, 'in solution,' give you new life?"[3]

An image of Mary Magdalene came to me: she was on a boat without oars, not knowing where the currents of the sea would take her. As I continued my own night sea journey, this vision opened the door to a new understanding. The image of the boat is a feminine symbol. I felt the presence of Mary Magdalene beside me, giving me support under my feet. She seemed to be saying: "Surrender yourself to what is happening, because it can open your soul to individual spiritual and cosmic vision. You will not achieve new spiritual values by using the oars of the ego's will to direct the journey; they are attainable only when the ego has surrendered its power. Abandon yourself to the spiritual cosmic power and the divine will talk to you." And it did!

The problem of contemporary humanity is that of having married only matter, as a unique reality. This brings struggle and abuse and the necessity to have more and more. On the other hand there are groups who dedicate themselves to pseudo-spiritual experiments and separate themselves completely from matter. The continuous political and social conflicts emerge from the division between matter and spirit within each person. This separation is the main problem of our time.

Scientists try hard to lift the mystery of matter only to recognize the indivisibility at the core of it. At a recent conference in Ascona,

Switzerland, physicist Wolfgang Pauli's concepts about body and spirit, unconventional for his time, were discussed. He believed in an undivided reality, which he defined in accordance with Jung as "unus mundus." For him, psyche and body were the representation of two aspects of this "One World."

But what has this to do with Mary Magdalene? Quite a lot has been written about her, and Dan Brown's book *The Da Vinci Code* generated an enormous resonance. This worldwide interest in Mary Magdalene reflects the longing of the human being to be whole again, to heal the separation that has been inflicted through religious and cultural traditions. She incarnates and is the expression of human wholeness, with no separation between her sexual nature and her spiritual nature. In her the opposites of male and female are united.

Mary Magdalene has been sent as a divine messenger, because the other Mary has not been understood in her feminine wholeness, only in her motherly and virginal aspect. The following cryptic words point in this direction:

> There were three who always walked with the Lord.
> Mary his mother; Mary, her sister; and Miriam of Magdala,
> Who was called his companion. For Miriam is his sister, his mother,
> and his companion. (Gospel of Philip)

Jean-Yves Leloup writes in his introduction to the *Gospel of Mary Magdalene:* "For this is a gospel that was at least inspired (if not literally written down) by a woman: Miriam of Magdala. Here she is neither the sinful woman of the canonical Gospels, nor the woman of more recent traditions that confuse her sin with some sort of misuse of the lively power of her sexuality. Here, she is the intimate friend of Yeshua, and the initiate who transmits his most subtle teachings."[4]

The controversy regarding the nature of Mary Magdalene's relationship with Jesus—as being physical or spiritual—is solved when we understand her as incorporating the sacred prostitute. She is an example of the most evident and effective aspects of the unity of matter and spirit. Through the physical sexual act the priestess of the Goddess expressed the sacred unity of matter and spirit and human and divine through her body. The word "prostitute" (sacred or not) has a negative connotation and immediately evokes sinful behavior as a result of a cultural-religious judgmental consciousness.

We need to understand Mary Magdalene on a symbolic level as an archetypal energy that can heal our inner laceration. Her central message seems to be:

> Overcome Duality
> because Matter and Spirit are
> ONE.

She teaches us how to accomplish this task in giving us "veiled instructions." According to the Gospels she anointed Jesus' head and feet. In Christian tradition the Holy Spirit and its gifts are symbolized by the holy oil. Giving oil and unguent represents the gift of our life substance, our love and respect, to something higher than the human. It is our recognition and honoring of the divine. Jung once wrote: "It is not so important to understand the other, more important is to recognize the divine in him." In this sense Mary Magdalene honored and loved the divine in Jesus. In anointing his feet, symbolizing matter, and his head, symbolizing spirit, she gave life substance to his soul and recognized in him the unity of matter and spirit.

The loving attention that has recently been given to the phenomenon of Mary Magdalene is analogous to anointing the divine in us that wants to incarnate. It doesn't matter in which form it has been expressed. What is important is that we anoint it with love.

Another veiled teaching Mary Magdalene gives us has to do with sin. Mark 16:9 says that Jesus "had cast seven devils" out of Mary Magdalene. In *The Gospel of Mary Magdalene,* Peter asks: "What is the sin of the world?" The teacher answers: "There is no sin. It is you who make sin exist when you act according to the habits of your corrupted nature; this is where sin lies." And more: "Attachment to matter gives rise to passion against nature."[5] In other words, we create sin when we separate matter from spirit. The seven devils have been interpreted in many ways. Seen symbolically, the image transmits a sense of our own inner and outer pollution. It is we who are attached to matter and who act against nature daily. It is we who need to be cleansed of our destructive dual thinking.

Mary Magdalene's central message is that we need to dissolve the contradictions that imprison us, to heal the divisions that deeply distress us. To do this, we need a loving, intimate relation between the masculine energy incorporated by Jesus and the feminine energy represented by Mary Magdalene. Mary Magdalene is the incarnated feminine aspect of the divine and in this sense she is the Daughter, as Jesus is the Son. Jesus' act of kissing her on the mouth, which is mentioned in the Gospels, symbolizes his canalization of his male loving energy into her.

Looking at the number of devils from this point of view reminds us that seven represents the addition of three (masculine) and four (feminine), respectively symbolizing sky and earth, and thus the totality of the universe. Jakob Boehme, the German mystic who studied number symbolism, affirms that the number seven represents the tension between the holy spiritual Trinity and the four terrestrial elements. We encounter seven in all cultures, myths, religions, legends, and fairy tales, and it is universally seen as a holy number.

I especially like the interpretation of St. Augustine, who remembers that in Genesis the six days of the week correspond to the work of creation, and the seventh day to rest. But then he adds that if the first seven numbers are related to what happens in time, eight corresponds to eternity. We therefore need to consider the eighth element, which would be "out of time." Like the number four, the number eight represents the totality. With eight we step out of the evolutionary process to enter an eternal condition. Eight is connected with love—love from and for the divine.

Love without end or beginning, as the figure eight suggests, is unconditional. Finally, love is the only force that heals, reconciles, and unites.

Eight indicates a passage from the known to the unknown. Eight means life after life; it points to the mystery of the Resurrection, which seems to contain all the teaching in its essence. Resurrection can also mean that we have to step out of conditional love to recollect and be connected again with divine unconditional love, with which we have been ever blessed. Resurrection could therefore be seen as awakening to eternity.

As the life cycle of Jesus was accomplished, Mary Magdalene was the first witness of his Resurrection, which Mark 16:9 also tells us: "Now when Jesus was risen early the first day of the week, he appeared first to Mary Magdalene." That means she was initiated in the mystery of life after life. The love between Mary Magdalene and Jesus becomes eternal as a manifestation of the Infinite (as Leloup calls it) in the very heart of our finitude, in this human space-time.

It is not by chance that Mary Magdalene is emerging now in our minds and souls. She is the Divine Messenger, Paraclete, Holy Ghost, midwife, guiding and protecting us to make the shift from an enormous cosmic cycle (soon coming to completion, according to many ancient spiritual traditions) to a new one. She is teaching us: "Do not fear, there is no death!" In this critical moment for humanity she helps us to enter into a new beginning, a new life with trust and love. She unites in herself all the many opposites that have been attributed to her, for the simple reason that she incorporates a *new consciousness,* which goes beyond all dualities. That is the real challenge she offers.

During my meditation on the symbolism of the number eight, a rare occurrence took place. There is a tiny brownish butterfly that has an extraordinary shape: it is an astonishing copy of a hummingbird. Its behavior is also like that of a hummingbird. The movement of its little wings forms an eight, and it can rest suspended in midair or shift horizontally or vertically with incredible speed. This movement between earth and sky evokes the image of a cross, acting as a mediator between above and below, matter and spirit. In fact, according to Mayan tradition, its energy or "medicine" can solve the contradiction of duality and brings love.

Although it is rarely seen, this butterfly always seems to appear at special moments in my life, coming as a messenger of love and as a mediator between the visible and the world beyond the veil, or in other words, between matter and spirit. It shows me that there is no separation, because it takes part of both and unites them in itself. This time it brought me the message that we are always in relation with the divine eternal love in us, symbolized by the eight—we only have to see and hear. And, like Mary Magdalene, we need to anoint it, give life substance, attention, and love to this connection to keep it alive. In one way or another it will materialize. In this case it came through a tiny butterfly, so similar to a hummingbird, which is also a symbol of the soul.

How could I—can we—not feel that Mary Magdalene is the veiled presence behind such messages?

How could I—can we—not feel blessed and thankful for her help?

Notes

INTRODUCTION

1. Barbara Walker, *The Woman's Encyclopedia of Myths and Secrets* (San Francisco: Harper and Row Publishers, 1983), 39.
2. T. S. Eliot, *Quattro quartetti* (Milano: Garzanti Editore, 1984), 78.
3. Marie-Louise von Franz, *Zahl und Zeit* (Stuttgart: E. Klett Verlag, 1970), 109.
4. Walker, *The Woman's Encyclopedia of Myths and Secrets*, 1048–49.
5. Nancy Qualls-Corbett, *The Sacred Prostitute: Eternal Aspect of the Feminine* (Toronto: Inner City Books, 1988), 30.
6. Richard Wilhelm, ed., *I Ging. Das Buch der Wandlungen* (München: Eugen Diederichs Verlag, 1956), 63n.
7. Anne Baring and Jules Cashford, *The Myth of the Goddess: Evolution of an Image* (London: Arkana Penguin Books, 1993), 24.

PART ONE
MYTHIC DIMENSIONS OF THE HISTORICAL PERIODS
OF THE FOUR WOMEN

1. C. G. Jung, *Psychology and Religion: West and East,* 2nd ed., Collected Works, Vol. 11, Bollingen Series XX (Princeton: Princeton University Press, 1989), 194, 190. (Original work published in 1958.)

CHAPTER ONE. THE PATRIARCHS

1. Mircea Eliade, *Storia delle credenze e delle idee religiose,* vol. 1 (Firenze: Sansoni Editore, 1979), 191. (Original work published in 1975.)
2. Ibid.
3. Baring and Cashford, *The Myth of the Goddess,* 443–44.
4. Eliade, *Storia delle credenze e delle idee religiose,* vol. 1, 192–93.
5. Ibid.
6. Walker, *The Woman's Encyclopedia of Myths and Secrets,* 271–72.
7. Eliade, *Storia delle credenze e delle idee religiose,* vol. 1, 192–193.

CHAPTER TWO. THE JUDGES

1. Jung, *Psychology and Religion,* 198–99.
2. Walker, *The Woman's Encyclopedia of Myths and Secrets,* 217.
3. Baring and Cashford, *The Myth of the Goddess,* 73.

CHAPTER THREE. PROPHETS AND KINGS

1. Marie-Louise von Franz, *Interpretation of Fairy Tales* (Zürich: Spring Publications, 1975), 121.
2. Personal communication from Christine Downing.
3. Helen M. Luke, *Kaleidoscope: "The Way of Woman" and Other Essays* (New York: Parabola Books, 1992), 258.
4. Ibid., 258–59.
5. Ibid., 26.
6. Ibid., 258–59.
7. Jung, *Psychology and Religion,* 198–99.
8. C. G. Jung, *Memories, Dreams, Reflections* (London-Glasgow: 1961), 327. (Original work published in 1961 under the title *Erinnerungen, Träume, Gedanken.*)

CHAPTER FOUR. THE FEMININE DIVINE AND THE RECLAIMING OF WHOLENESS

1. Walker, *The Woman's Encyclopedia of Myths and Secrets,* 38–39.
2. Jung, *Psychology and Religion,* 175, 167.

CHAPTER FIVE.
TAMAR, THE SACRED PROSTITUTE

1. Walker, *The Woman's Encyclopedia of Myths and Secrets,* 764.
2. Jung, *Mysterium Coniunctionis,* Collected Works, vol. 14. Bollingen Series XX (Princeton: Princeton University Press, 1963), 71n.
3. Baring and Cashford, *The Myth of the Goddess,* 496.
4. Ibid., 197.
5. Erich Neumann, *Zur Psychologie des Weiblichen* (Zürich: Rascher Verlag, 1953), 25.
6. von Franz, *Interpretation of Fairy Tales,* 91.
7. Ibid., 90.
8. Ibid., 140.
9. Ibid., 178.
10. Ariel Spilsbury and Michael Bryner, *The Mayan Oracle: Return Path to the Stars* (Santa Fe, N.M.: Bear & Company, 1992), 136.
11. Martin Prechtel, *Secrets of the Talking Jaguar: A Mayan Shaman's Journey to the Heart of the Indigenous Soul* (New York: Jeremy P. Tarcher, Putnam, 1998), 169–70.
12. *Helvetas* (1998), Issue No. 153.
13. Caitlín Matthews, *Sophia Goddess of Wisdom: The Divine Feminine from Black Goddess to World-Soul* (London: Aquarian/Thorsons, 1992), 54.

CHAPTER SIX. RAHAB, THE MERETRIX

1. Jung, *Psychology and Religion,* 209.
2. Baring and Cashford, *The Myth of the Goddess,* 630.
3. Ibid., 273.
4. Ibid., 480.
5. Ibid., 294.
6. Ibid., 285.
7. Ibid., 74.
8. Ibid., 72.
9. Ibid., 283–84.
10. Ibid., 283.
11. Ibid., 442.

12. Ibid., 284.

13. C. G. Jung, *Alchemical Studies,* Collected Works, vol. 13, Bollingen Series XX (Princeton: Princeton University Press, 1967), 25–26.

14. Raphael Patai, *The Hebrew Goddess,* 3rd ed. (Detroit: Wayne State University Press, 1990), 39. (Original work published in 1967.)

15. Karl Kerényi, *Humanistische Seelenforschung* (München-Wien: Langen Müller, 1966), 343.

16. Ibid., 342.

17. Ibid., 355–56.

CHAPTER SEVEN. RUTH, REDEEMING THE SOUL

1. Rumi, *The Essential Rumi* (London: Penguin Books, 1995), 15.

2. Baring and Cashford, *The Myth of the Goddess,* 364.

3. Angeles Arrien, *The Tarot Handbook: Practical Applications of Ancient Visual Symbols* (Sonoma: Arcus Publishing Company, 1987), 33–34.

4. Baring and Cashford, *The Myth of the Goddess,* 610.

5. Walker, *The Woman's Encyclopedia of Myths and Secrets,* 585.

6. Baring and Cashford, *The Myth of the Goddess,* 444–46.

7. Lois C. Dubin, "Fullness and Emptiness, Fertility and Loss: Meditations on Naomi's Tale in the Book of Ruth," in Judith A. Kates and Gail Twersky Reimer, eds., *Reading Ruth: Contemporary Women Reclaim a Sacred Story* (New York: Ballantine Books, 1994), 142–43.

CHAPTER EIGHT. BATHSHEBA, THE UNFINISHED STORY OR THE DAUGHTER OF THE GODDESS

1. Walker, *The Woman's Encyclopedia of Myths and Secrets,* 1100.

2. Baring and Cashford, *The Myth of the Goddess,* 286.

PART THREE
THE CONCEPTION OF MARY: A SYMBOLIC INTERPRETATION OF THE APOCRYPHAL LEGEND

1. Marie-Louise von Franz, *Problems of the Feminine in Fairytales,* revised edition (Irving, Tex.: Spring Publications, Inc., 1972), 21. (Original work published in 1970.)

CHAPTER NINE. THE PARENTS OF MARY

1. James Hillman, *The Force of Character and the Lasting Life* (New York: Ballantine Books, 1999), 190.

EPILOGUE
MARY MAGDALENE—THE SOUL-TEACHER
IN THE NEW TESTAMENT

1. Baring and Cashford, *The Myth of the Goddess,* 629.
2. Anna Maria Bona, ed., *Maddalena l'Altra Metà di Cristo,* Milano: Melchisedek, 2007, 182–183.
3. Thomas Moore, *Dark Nights of the Soul* (New York: Gotham Books, 2004), 68.
4. Jean-Yves Leloup, *The Gospel of Mary Magdalene* (Rochester, Vt.: Inner Traditions, 2002), 6–7.
5. Ibid., 25.

Bibliography

Arrien, Angeles. *The Tarot Handbook: Practical Applications of Ancient Visual Symbols.* Sonoma: Arcus Publishing Company, 1987.

Baring, Anne, and Jules Cashford. *The Myth of the Goddess: Evolution of an Image.* London: Arkana Penguin Books, 1993.

Buonaiuti, Ernesto. *Maria und die jungfräuliche Geburt Jesu.* In Olga Fröbe-Kapteyn (Hrsg.), *Eranos Jahrbuch* 1938, Band VI. Zürich: Rhein Verlag, 1939.

Campbell, Joseph. *Von der Geistigen Natur des Mythos.* In T. Lehner, ed., Keltisches Bewusstsein (28). München: Dianus Trikont Verlag, 1985. (Original work published in 1982 in R. O'Driscoll, ed., *The Celtic Consciousness.*)

———. *The Power of Myth.* New York: Doubleday Publishers, 1988.

Conforto, Giuliana. *Il gioco cosmico dell'uomo.* Edizioni Noesis, 1998.

Craveri, Marcello (cura). *I Vangeli apocrifi.* Torino: Einaudi, 1969.

Die heilige Schrift. Die in Zürich kirchlich eingeführte Uebersetzung aufs neue nach dem Grundtext berichtigt. Im Auftrag der zürcherischen Kirchensynode herausgegeben vom Kirchenrat des Kantons Zürich. Zürich: Reutimann & Co., 1932.

Dubin, Lois C. "Fullness and Emptiness, Fertility and Loss: Meditations on Naomi's Tale in the Book of Ruth." In Judith A. Kates and Gail Twersky Reimer, eds., *Reading Ruth: Contemporary Women Reclaim a Sacred Story* (New York: Ballantine Books, 1994).

Eliade, Mircea. *Storia delle credenze e delle idee religiose,* vol. 1. Firenze: Sansoni Editore, 1979. (Original work published in 1975 under the title *A History of Religious Ideas.*)

Eliot, T. S. *Quattro quartetti.* Italy: Garzanti Editore, 1984. (Original work published 1959 under the title *Four Quartets.*)

Fox, Matthew, and Rupert Sheldrake. *Engel, die kosmische Intelligenz.* München: Kösel, 1998. (Original work published 1996 under the title *The Physics of Angels: A Realm Where Spirit and Science Meet.*)

Franz, Marie-Louise von. *A Psychological Interpretation of the Golden Ass of Apuleius.* New York: Spring Publications, 1970.

———. *Zahl und Zeit.* Stuttgart: E. Klett Verlag, 1970.

———. *Problems of the Feminine in Fairytales,* revised ed. Irving, Tex.: Spring Publications, Inc., 1972. (Original work published in 1970.)

———. *Shadow and Evil in Fairy Tales.* Zürich: Spring Publications, 1974.

———. *Interpretation of Fairy Tales.* Zürich: Spring Publications, 1975.

———. *Individuation in Fairy Tales.* Zürich: Spring Publications, 1977.

———. *Die Erlösung des Weiblichen im Manne.* Frankfurt am Main: Insel Verlag, 1980. (Original work published in 1970 under the title *A Psychological Interpretation of the Golden Ass of Apuleius.*)

———. *Il femminile nella fiaba.* Torino: Editore Boringhieri, 1983.

———. *Alchemia.* Torino: Editore Boringhieri, 1984. (Original work published under the title *Alchemy.*)

Gimbutas, Marija. *The Language of the Goddess.* San Francisco: Harper, 1989.

Gorion, Micha Josef bin. *Die Sagen der Juden.* Frankfurt am Main: Insel Verlag, 1962.

Helvetas. Issue no. 153, 1998.

Hillman, James. *The Force of Character and the Lasting Life.* New York: Ballantine Books, 1999.

The Holy Bible, the authorized King James version. This version is cited textually unless otherwise stated.

Jung, C. G. *Memories, Dreams, Reflections.* London: Glasgow, 1961.

——. *Mysterium Coniunctionis.* Collected Works, vol. 14. Bollingen Series XX. Princeton: Princeton University Press, 1963.

——. *Alchemical Studies.* Collected Works, vol. 13. Bollingen Series XX. Princeton: Princeton University Press, 1967.

——. *Aion,* 2nd ed. Collected Works, vol. 9 (II). Bollingen Series XX. Princeton: Princeton University Press, 1968.

——. *The Structure and Dynamics of the Psyche,* 2nd ed. Collected Works, vol. 8. Bollingen Series XX. Princeton: Princeton University Press, 1969.

——. *Psychology and Alchemy,* 2nd ed. Collected Works, vol. 12. Bollingen Series XX. Princeton: Princeton University Press, 1977.

——. *Psychology and Religion: West and East,* 2nd ed. Collected Works, vol. 11. Bollingen Series XX. Princeton: Princeton University Press, 1989.

Jung, Emma, and Marie-Louise von Franz. *The Grail Legend.* London: Hodder & Stoughton, 1971. (Original work published in 1960 under the title *Die Graalslegende in psychologischer Sicht.*)

Kerényi, Karl. *Humanistische Seelenforschung.* München-Wien: Langen Müller, 1966.

——. *Dionysos. Urbild des unzerstörbaren Lebens.* München-Wien: Langen Müller, 1976.

La Bibbia. *Nuovissima versione dai testi originali.* Milano: Edizioni San Paolo, 1997. *La Sacra Bibbia.* Tradotta dai Testi originali con note, a cura del Pontificio Istituto Biblico di Roma. Roma: Casa Editrice Adriano Salani, 1961.

Laffont, R., ed. *Dictionnaire des symboles,* 2nd ed. Paris: Editions Robert Laffont S.A. et Editions Jupiter, 1982. (Original work published in 1969.)

Leloup, Jean-Yves. *The Gospel of Mary Magdalene.* Rochester, Vt.: Inner Traditions, 2002.

Luke, Helen M. *Kaleidoscope: "The Way of Woman" and Other Essays.* New York: Parabola Books, 1992.

——. *The Way of Woman.* New York: Double Day, 1995.

Matthews, Caitlín. *Sophia Goddess of Wisdom: The Divine Feminine from Black Goddess to World-Soul.* London: Aquarian/Thorsons, 1992.

Moore, Thomas. *Dark Nights of the Soul.* New York: Gotham Books, 2004.

Neumann, Erich. *Zur Psychologie des Weiblichen*. Zürich: Rascher Verlag, 1953.

———. *Die grosse Mutter. Der Archetyp des grossen Weiblichen*. Zürich: Rhein-Verlag, 1956.

Nola, Alfonso M. di (cura). *Vangeli apocrifi Natività e infanzia*. Milan: Guanda, 1977.

Odelain, O., and R. Séguineau. *Lexikon der biblischen Eigennamen*. Düsseldorf: Patmos Verlag, 1981. (Original work published under the title *Dictionnaire des noms propres de la Bible*.)

Patai, Raphael. *The Hebrew Goddess*, 3rd ed. Detroit: Wayne State University Press, 1990. (Original work published in 1967.)

Prechtel, Martin. *Secrets of the Talking Jaguar. A Mayan Shaman's Journey to the Heart of the Indigenous Soul*. New York: Jeremy P. Tarcher, Putnam, 1998.

Ranke-Graves, Robert von. *Die Weisse Göttin. Sprache des Mythos*. Reinbek bei Hamburg: Rowohlt Taschenbuch Verlag GmbH, 1981. (Original work published in 1948 under the title *The White Goddess*.)

Ranke-Graves, Robert von, and Raphael Patai. Hebräische Mythologie. *Über die Schöpfungsgeschichte und andere Mythen aus dem Alten Testament*. Reinbek bei Hamburg: Rowohlt Taschenbuch Verlag GmbH, 1986. (Original work published in 1963 under the title *Hebrew Books: The Book of Genesis*.)

Rumi. *The Essential Rumi*. London: Penguin Books, 1995.

Spilsbury, A., and M. Bryner. *The Mayan Oracle: Return Path to the Stars*. Santa Fe: Bear & Company, 1992.

Voragine, Jacobus de. *Die Legenda Aurea*. Translated from the Latin by Richard Benz. Köln & Olten: Verlag Jakob Segner, 1955. (Original work published ca. 1292.)

Walker, Barbara. *The Woman's Encyclopedia of Myths and Secrets*. San Francisco: Harper and Row Publishers, 1983.

Warlick, M. E. *Le Pietre Filosofali*. Milano: Gruppo Editoriale Armenia S.p.A., 1998. (Original work published in 1997 under the title *The Philosopher's Stone*.)

Wilhelm, Richard, ed. *I Ging. Das Buch der Wandlungen*. München: Eugen Diederichs Verlag, 1956.

Wolf, Christa. *Medea*. Germany: Luchterhand, 1996.

Index

BOOKS OF RELATED INTEREST

The Woman with the Alabaster Jar
Mary Magdalen and the Holy Grail
by Margaret Starbird

The Goddess in the Gospels
Reclaiming the Sacred Feminine
by Margaret Starbird

Mary Magdalene, Bride in Exile
by Margaret Starbird

Magdalene's Lost Legacy
Symbolic Numbers and the Sacred Union in Christianity
by Margaret Starbird

The Gospel of Mary Magdalene
by Jean-Yves Leloup

Kabbalistic Teachings of the Female Prophets
The Seven Holy Women of Ancient Israel
by J. Zohara Meyerhoff Hieronimus

The Church of Mary Magdalene
The Sacred Feminine and the Treasure of Rennes-le-Château
by Jean Markale

The Virgin Mary Conspiracy
The True Father of Christ and the Tomb of the Virgin
by Graham Phillips

INNER TRADITIONS • BEAR & COMPANY
P.O. Box 388
Rochester, VT 05767
1-800-246-8648
www.InnerTraditions.com

Or contact your local bookseller